Is This What Re...

A novel by

Vernon Coleman

**The amazing secret of Elvis Presley's faked death.
And what he did after he died.**

Could it have happened like this?

This book is copyright. Enquiries should be addressed to the publisher.
This book was first published under the title 'My Secret Years with Elvis Presley' and the pen name Tim Wood.

Copyright © Vernon Coleman 2014

The moral right of Vernon Coleman to be identified as the author of this work has been asserted in accordance with the Copyright, Designs and Patents Act 1988. All rights reserved.

Introduction

With the help of his father, Vernon Presley, and his manager, Colonel Tom Parker, singing legend Elvis Presley faked his own death and moved to Paris. Exhausted by the interminable demands of fans, and aware that his responses to the stress of superstardom were killing him, Presley wanted a new life. Parker approved the fake death because he reckoned it was Elvis's best available career move – guaranteed to boost sales of records and memorabilia. This is the story of what happened next. Don't believe it? Read this book. You will. I'm the only other person alive to know Elvis's secret, and the man who shared Elvis's second life in Paris, France.

Foreword

There will almost certainly be some who will say 'I didn't know about any of this and so it cannot be true'. People who were close to Elvis, either because they were related to him or because they worked for him, may insist that Elvis Presley died when everyone thinks he died, in the bathroom at Graceland back in 1977. That's what everyone was expected to believe and I still feel a small sense of pride in the fact that we pulled things off so successfully. Only five people knew that Elvis didn't die on the 16th of August in 1977. One of the five died that day. And two died a few years afterwards. Today there are only the two of us, Elvis and myself, who know the whole truth. For Elvis those times were an emotional roller coaster and there were many days when I never thought we would succeed. There have been many down days but, fortunately, there have been slightly more up days. Occasionally, the hours have dragged but the years have flashed by. Some of the details of what happened are hazy and neither Elvis nor I can remember everything that happened to us. I don't want to make things up so occasionally this story becomes a little fuzzy in the detail.

    Today, we both live in Paris, where we have lived for over a third of a century and, all things considered, we are both in pretty good health. Both of us can still walk, talk and read and Elvis can still charm the ladies as well as he ever could. We have apartments close to each other and see or speak every day. My hearing isn't what it was and some days, when his hip is playing him up, Elvis walks with a black ebony cane with a silver band around the handle but neither of us has any complaints about the cards we've been dealt. Paris is a good city in which to live when you are old. The elderly are well-respected and well-treated; they go for walks, they play boules, they exercise their dogs, they sit in cafés where they are known by name, and where their favourite table will often be reserved for them and on occasion they may even enjoy a quiet drink at the bar. Frenchmen who are retired dress with dignity and no French woman would ever dream of leaving her apartment without putting on her make-up and a decent dress. Women in their seventies, eighties and even nineties still visit the hairdresser once a week where they will, of course, also have their fingernails attended to. The elderly in France do not wear elasticated trousers, live in ghettoes where they can be forgotten or travel around on coach trips. Paris is, in short, a good place to be old.

Elvis gave me his full approval to write this account of what happened on the sole condition that I include an apology from him to everyone who mourned his passing. We both hope that everyone who reads this book will understand why we did what we did and accept that even now, so many years later, we really don't think there was a choice.

I hope that fans and journalists will respect Elvis's request that he be allowed to keep his new found privacy and to live out his final years in the peace and happiness his new life has given him.

Dedication
To my darling Donna Antoinette with all my love.

Chapter One

I sat at a table at the back of the Deux Magots terrace in Saint Germain des Pres and watched as he threaded his way between the café tables. Deux Magots is one of the smartest and best known cafés in Paris. Jean-Paul Sartre, James Joyce, Pablo Picasso, Albert Camus and Ernest Hemingway were all regular customers. He was better known than any of them but no one looked at him. A few people shuffled their chairs forwards an inch or two to make space for him to pass. But no one stared; no one actually looked at him; no one recognised the man who had, less than a year earlier, been unable to leave the house without an entourage that would have satisfied an Emperor and without being followed by a small army of fans and a herd of reporters and photographers. He had one of the most famous faces on the planet but here in Paris he seemed no more visible than the rest of us. No cosmetic surgeon had touched his skin but today he was just one of the crowd, gathered together out of the winter chill. He was not forgotten but he was unrecognised and, therefore ignored. I couldn't help feeling rather pleased with what we had achieved.

It was raining yet again and cold enough for the snow promised by the heavy sky. At six feet three inches he was taller than most men (we couldn't make him shorter but shoes with heel lifts had made it easy to add a couple of inches to his height) and at 160 pounds he was now considerably slimmer than most men approaching the foothills of middle age. The crash diet had been easier than either of us had thought it would be, and just as successful as we had hoped, and he was now no heavier than he had been in his prime. The famous hips were no longer covered in thick ripples of lard, as they had been the last time he'd been seen in public.

There had been other changes too. Thanks to contact lenses the famous blue eyes were now brown. He'd worn brown contact lenses in a few of his early movies so he found them easy to wear. Even hard-line fans were always surprised at this. Some had even questioned whether contact lenses existed back in the late 1950's but the truth is that they were invented by Leonardo da Vinci in 1508 and had been pretty widely used even back then. We'd toyed with the idea of green lenses but had decided against them simply because green eyes are too noticeable. What remained of his hair, now cut short and styled in a rather ordinary right to left style, was entirely hidden under a woollen, Irish flat cap which he wore every time he left the apartment. In the summer we'd switch it for something lighter and more suitable; a panama perhaps. It still amazed me how much you could change someone's appearance without resorting to the horrors of cosmetic surgery. The iconic sideburns had gone, of course and the shape of those oh too famous lips were disguised by a fashionable and luxuriant Zapata moustache.

After being with him every day for just over six months I'd pretty well got into the habit of calling him Jesse without feeling as though I were acting in one of the thirty odd damned movies the Colonel had forced him to make. And some of the time I even thought of him as Jesse, though to be honest I found it a bit spooky and wished he'd stuck with the name on his new passport. It was, I suppose, his one way of holding onto some small fragment of the past. We were careful not to use the name Jesse in public (though to be honest I don't think it would have been too much of a risk) and on the couple of occasions when I'd used it in front of other people it had been easy to brush aside. 'Just a silly private joke, an old nickname,' I said, when I used it in front of a nice Scottish couple we met in Fouquet's restaurant on the Champs Elysées one Sunday afternoon.

It hadn't been as difficult for me as it had been for him, of course, but they certainly hadn't been an easy few months for either of us.

The first few days had, without a doubt, been by far the worst. We were still in the States then, of course, and together we had watched the coverage of his death and the funeral on television. Those were the darkest, most difficult days we've ever had in exile together. Several times I thought the whole thing was going to fall apart and we were going to end up disgraced and quite probably in prison. None of us had been quite sure whether or not pretending to be dead was a criminal offence but I was pretty sure some ambitious district attorney somewhere would have been able to think of something with which to charge us.

There had been a good deal of anger and not a few tears and I'm damned sure that if he'd had a gun he would have shot a hole in the television screen. People who would have never dared to utter a word of criticism while he'd been alive had vied with one another to spew acid on his memory. I couldn't believe some of the things that were said by people I'd regarded as his friends. I take my hat off to him for the way he got through that.

He'd wanted to bring the gun with him to France but I'd said 'No'. Things were complicated enough without having to obtain fake permits for a hand gun. I'd managed to prise the damned thing out of his hand by promising that I'd buy him one to celebrate the first twelve month anniversary of his new life. It was a 9 mm Smith and Wesson and I'd wiped it clean of fingerprints (well, you never know, do you?) and tossed the damned thing into a river from a bridge I couldn't take you to it if you offered to pay me. All I can remember is that it was somewhere in Kentucky. At least I'm pretty sure it was Kentucky. Two days after I'd got rid of that one I found a Colt .45 sitting on the toilet cistern of the bathroom we were sharing. That one, also well wiped, went into another river. Later, in New York, I took a derringer and a 0.25 automatic off him. That was the only time we've ever had a row. I told him I'd walk out on him if he had any more guns hidden away. I've never seen him look as embarrassed or as ashamed as he was that day. Afterward, we hugged like brothers and we've never had a problem since then. I don't believe there are many friends who have as good a relationship as we have. Damnit, I don't believe there are many happily married couples who get on as well as we do – particularly when you consider the exceptional and stressful circumstances.

It was only when he arrived at the table where I was sitting that I noticed that he was carrying his guitar case. He had been busking again. In our early months in Paris, I really hated it when he went busking. He didn't open his mouth, of course, he just played the guitar. But I was still terrified that one day he'd forget and start singing.

Chapter Two

Elvis and I had known each other, on and off, for quite a while when we decided that it was time for him to die. Colonel Parker and Vernon Presley, Elvis's father, were surprisingly keen on the idea. They were a pretty ruthless, disreputable pair who had both lived their lives a considerable distance from the straight and narrow though only Vernon could speak of prison food with the benefit of personal experience. The Colonel was always the one with the eye for the big ideas. Lots of people said rough things about the Colonel but the one thing I will say for him is that he always thought big. And he was never scared of doing something no one else would even dream of doing. He was thinking laterally long before anyone else.

The truth is that Elvis's life had become unbearable. He had not been able to go out in public for years and was probably one of only half a dozen people on the planet who could not go shopping, enjoy a walk in the park, attend a sports event or go to the cinema without being surrounded by aides, bodyguards and throngs of well-wishers. Members of royal families are trained for this sort of social loneliness but Elvis had not been prepared for it and it bothered him a good deal. In private he frequently referred to himself as a prisoner of his own fame and he knew that many of those who were close to him were faking their affection. Everyone wanted to meet Elvis. Everyone wanted to be his 'friend'.

And to make things worse he found that the pressure of performing, and satisfying both the press and the fans, had become intolerable. As he grew older he found the stress of expectation growing rather than shrinking. Every performance had to be at least as good as, and preferably better than, the one before. He became irritable, easily angered, moody and quite often profoundly depressed. He found comfort in eating and, inevitably, gained a good deal of weight. Naturally, that just made everything worse. He had special stage costumes made to disguise the fact that he could no longer move easily and gracefully but there is only so much that can be done with tassels and clever cutting and eventually not even the skill of the costume designers could hide the fact that that the once legendary hips were now lost amidst an acre of flab and his movements, once so fluid and cat-like, were now slow and creaky.

It was, I think, the French Nobel prize winning writer Albert Camus who claimed that most of us feel a strange sense of dissatisfaction with our own lives because, although our lives appear to us, from the inside, to be chaotic, incoherent and intrinsically unmanageable, other people's lives appear to be complete, whole, well-managed and enviably neat and tidy. This, of course, is because although we see everything in our own lives we usually only see other people's lives from afar. The time I had spent with Elvis had convinced me that Camus had been talking through his beret. Compared to Elvis's life my own sojourn on earth was a model of sanity and predictability. It seemed to me that it was nothing short of a miracle that Elvis was still managing to function at all. He had started his working life as a truck driver and had become, quite possibly, the most famous person on the planet. He was, without a doubt, the most successful entertainer in history and he had (with the aid of a fairground huckster) somehow succeeded in becoming more royal than any Royal on earth. Every move he made, every favour he bestowed or withheld, every utterance, was studied, reviewed and subjected to endless criticism. He had unasked for responsibilities for a vast army of employees and their families and for hundreds of millions of fickle and judgemental fans who had vast and unprecedented expectations. His soul was effectively owned by whole flocks of strangers. It would have been too much for an insensitive psychopath to deal with; for a sensitive individual the success had become a daily nightmare. It was no wonder that he ate too much and relied on drugs. The more he was criticised, and the greater the expectation became, the more he ate and the more drugs he took. The fatter he got the more he was criticised. He had entered a vicious downward spiral from which there seemed, at first glance, to be no escape.

There was, he told me very late one evening, only one answer. He had to disappear. The old life had to be cast aside, like a snake's skin, and a new life allowed to grow from within.

`I eat too much and take too many pills because I'm stressed all the time,' he told me. `I'm too fat and too tired to tour. I can't stand being me any longer. I hate the critics, the reviewers, the journalists and the book writers. The more they say bad things about me the more I eat and the more drugs I take. It's a vicious circle, man. I'm becoming a joke. My little girl will grow up to know her father as a fat idiot, laughed at by people. The memory of who I was will be tarnished by what I've become.'

Two things were making things far worse than they need have been. First, there was the Colonel's endless insistence that Elvis continue performing. Parker owed huge sums of money to hoteliers in Las Vegas and at the time these weren't the sort of people who were happy to put IOUs into a drawer and wait until they matured. They wanted their money now and they wanted it with interest and in cash. Elvis was the Colonel's 'Get Out Of Jail Free' card (or, perhaps more accurately, his 'Avoid Having Your Legs Broken' card).

Elvis felt an enormous sense of responsibility to the people who had learned to rely upon him and the Colonel took advantage of this and when Elvis said he didn't want to do any more shows he was quick to remind him just how many people relied upon him for their weekly pay cheques. The cost of running the Elvis empire was absurd and his monthly expenses were astronomical. There were plenty of small towns in America surviving very nicely, thank you, on less income than Elvis had coming in but he was always hard up. The Colonel never seemed to worry about money. He always assumed that there would be another tour, another record, another successful piece of merchandise, another film, another deal. But Elvis did worry. He worried that there wouldn't be enough money available to provide for his daughter, his father and the huge family of Presley's, friends, staff and hangers on who had come to rely on the King for their regular supply of Lincolns and Cadillacs, and to provide them with the champagne lifestyle to which they had become accustomed.

The second problem was that two former friends of Elvis's, Red and Sonny, had written a book about him. Red and Sonny had been close friends who'd lived with Elvis at Graceland and they knew where all the bodies were buried. The Colonel had acquired an advance copy of the book and had, unwisely, given it to Elvis to read. Elvis was so upset with the pair of former friends, whom he had trusted, that he wanted to shoot them both and bury their bodies somewhere in the grounds. If the Colonel had let him he probably would have done just that. The book came out just a couple of weeks before Elvis officially died but Elvis read what they had to say some time before that and I know for a fact that he cried for days over what they had written. He was upset by the betrayal and believed that the book would finish his career but he was also upset at the thought that his little girl, Lisa, would read the book when she grew up. The darned book made it difficult for him to trust new people and to be honest it's easy to understand why.

The result of all this was that Elvis was desperate to retire.

He insisted that he wouldn't miss the adulation because the price was too high and he simply couldn't pay it any more. 'I want a less stressful life,' he said. 'I look at these guys with ordinary lives and I envy them. I know they probably envy me but I envy them back. I'd give anything to live a simple, honest life and to get away from all this stuff.' He talked, with remarkable naivety, of giving up show business completely and becoming an ordinary citizen. He was so desperate to escape from the world in which he lived that he was prepared to give up Graceland and move into something smaller and less expensive.

'You could never do it,' was my first reaction. 'You're too famous, too well-known. If you gave up all this you'd have to change your life completely. It would be like going into the Witness Protection Programme. You'd never again be able to see Lisa Marie or Vernon.' In fact, I thought we would need something better than the FBI's Witness Protection Programme. Elvis would need a genuine new identity, provided by another Government, and he would need to live in a different country.

'I can change,' insisted Elvis. 'I could lose weight and give up the pills. Without worrying myself sick about the next concert, and whether or not the next record is going to be a hit, I could do it.'

I thought about it for a few moments. It was, it seemed, just one of those late night conversations that people have when they're too tired to think straight but are playing around with some impossible dream. 'You'd never be able to tell anyone,' I said. 'No one. Ever.'

'I could do it,' said Elvis. He put down the peanut and jelly sandwich he'd been eating and leant forward. 'You'll have to come with me. I need you with me. I couldn't trust anyone else.'

'Where would you go? You're far too well-known to live in the States.'

Elvis thought for a while.

'I'll go to Paris, France,' he said. 'I like Paris. We had some good times there didn't we?' He smiled and his eyes lit up. It was as if someone had turned on a 1000 watt bulb inside his head. I have never met anyone with a better smile than Elvis. It was the one thing I'd never been able to disguise about him. Even today, nearly 40 years after his official 'death', the smile is still there. The cheeks dimple, the mouth twists up a little, the head goes slightly forward and to one side and there it is: a million dollar smile that any politician in the world would sell his soul to possess for just one election campaign.

When Elvis had served as a GI in Germany he had spent much of his R and R time in Paris. That was where we had met. My career as a writer had hit the buffers and I'd been working as a public relations executive for one of the big nightclubs. My normal job was to make sure that the club's name was mentioned in the papers when celebrities visited. If a film star such as John-Paul Belmondo or Alain Delon came into the club the manager wanted to see pictures in all the papers and the weekly magazines. With Elvis it was different. My job was to keep his visits as secret as possible. This was in the club's interests as much as his. The Colonel didn't like it being known that his 'boy' had been seen ogling the girls in an up-market strip club. And the club's management didn't like the fact that on the two occasions when it had became known that Elvis was in the club there had, within an hour, been such a big crowd in the street outside that paying customers hadn't been able to force their way through to reach the door.

'You'd have to tell the Colonel that you're retiring,' I pointed out. Colonel Tom Parker had managed Elvis since they'd met at the beginning of 1955. Elvis believed that he owed his success to Parker's single-minded dedication and he trusted him implicitly. By now he was paying the Colonel a huge part of his income and I wasn't the one who thought that was a rather large part of Elvis's problem. When you took expenses and taxes out of what was left Elvis was nowhere near as rich as he should have been and nowhere near as rich as people thought he was. Elvis could never understand why he was always broke and had to keep working in order to pay the bills but the explanation wasn't difficult to find.

'You tell him for me,' said Elvis, who respected the Colonel so much that he was always a little in awe of him. 'You tell him.'

Many people run and hide from something they have done (or not done) or from the person they have been and the life they have made for themselves. For most of them the running and the hiding are not too difficult. I knew that for Elvis the running and the hiding would be almost impossibly difficult. And I suspected, and hoped, that by the morning he would have forgotten the conversation.

But Elvis didn't forget.

And when I was having breakfast the following morning he came and sat down beside me, looked around to make sure that there was no one in earshot, and asked me when I intended to tell the Colonel what we were planning.

'It won't work,' I told him. 'You're just too damned famous. The minute people realise that you're not at Graceland and not on the road they'll want to know where you are. Every journalist in the world will be looking for you. Not to mention several million fans. You'd have to hide in a cellar or an attic somewhere and what sort of life would that be? You'd be far worse off than you are now.'

'I've got to do it,' said Elvis. He looked as disappointed as a child who's been told that Christmas has been postponed indefinitely. It was at that moment that I realised just how near the edge he was. There were genuine tears in his eyes and he looked old and worn out. 'I can't go on like this,' he whispered. I can still remember his words and I can still remember the anguish in his voice. It was real. I've always thought that Elvis was a better actor than the films he made but if he'd been that good an actor there would have been little golden statuettes all over the mansion. 'I'm on a treadmill, man. I got to get off. I'd rather be dead than carry on like this.' He paused. 'Besides, I've got to get away from the death threats.'

'The death threats! What death threats? Are they serious?' Even in the 1970's all really famous people received death threats, but very few were taken seriously by anyone, often including the people making them. But Elvis sounded very serious. And it was the first I'd heard of it.

'We've been getting threats,' said Elvis. 'They sound pretty serious. They've even threatened to kill Lisa. If I were dead there wouldn't be any point in them making threats, would there?'

We sat in silence for a few moments. Finally, I spoke. 'That's the only way to do it?'

He looked across at me.'To die?' He frowned. 'You mean I should kill myself? Or are you going to do it for me? Either way that's a sin. I ain't going to kill myself.'

I shook my head. 'I don't mean that you should die. Not for real. Just that maybe you should pretend to die.'

He looked at me and frowned. 'Just tell people I'd died?'

'No one would look for you if they thought you were dead. There'd have to be a body and a funeral. But you could disappear if the press and the fans were all convinced that you were lying in a coffin under six feet of earth. Why would anyone bother to look for you when everyone already thought they knew where you were?'

'I don't know,' said Elvis shaking his head. 'What are we going to tell Lisa Marie? How are we going to explain to her that Daddy is just pretending to be dead? Or does she have to pretend to die? And Ginger? And the Colonel? And my dad? And Billy? If we all die at the same time folk are going to be suspicious. And if they know I'm still alive, and not really dead, they'll give it away. And if I'm living in Philadelphia and Lisa Marie and Ginger and the Colonel and everyone come visiting, someone is going to smell a rat. Someone at some paper is going to want to know why everyone I knew is now suddenly living in some new place they probably never even visited before. And that someone is going to want to know the name of the big fat guy in the dark glasses who hangs around with them.'

'We can't tell them,' I said. 'We can't tell anyone. Except maybe the Colonel. Everyone else has to really believe that you've died.' I knew the Colonel would see the advantages immediately. He would see it as Elvis's best career option. Whenever well-known recording artists die their record and memorabilia sales go through the roof.

'No, no, no,' said Elvis. He stood up and shook his head. 'I can't do that. It wouldn't work. And I can't do it.' He had gone a deathly shade of grey and I genuinely thought he was going to have a heart attack. He looked terrible. He really was in awful shape in those days and I believe that if he'd done the series of shows that the Colonel had planned for him he would have died for real – probably live on stage – and Elvis would have left the building for the last time on a gurney.

I stood up and helped him sit back down. He looked twenty years older than he was and no life insurance salesman would have sold him a policy the way he looked that day.

'OK,' I said. 'Forget it. But it's the only way.'

'I can't do it,' repeated Elvis.

We sat for a minute or two. Neither of us spoke. Slowly, his colour came back. When he looked a little less like a statue and a little more like a human being likely to live long enough to eat it I went to the kitchen and ordered some breakfast for him. I honestly didn't think he'd mention my idea again. Outside the kitchen I tossed a coin, having decided that if it came down 'heads' I would refuse to have anything to do with his plan even if he did decide to go ahead with it. When the coin showed 'heads' it had rolled under a chair and since, as everyone knows, the result of a tossed coin is invalid if the coin has rolled under a piece of furniture, I tossed it a second time. It showed heads again and since it didn't seem right to make a decision based on a replacement toss I tossed the coin a third time. This time it landed tails up and I decided that I wouldn't do or say anything, or make any decisions, but would wait to see if Elvis mentioned the idea again., I spent the rest of the morning trying to think of a way that I could persuade the Colonel not to make Elvis go to Las Vegas.

Chapter Three

'How would this dying thing work?' asked Elvis, later that evening. His speech was slow because of the drugs. The damned pills he was taking had slowed down his thinking and his talking and had wrecked his memory. In the old days he never forgot anything. These days he even forgot songs he had sung a hundred times. He'd start a song and then be reduced to humming. On stage he sometimes relied on band members reminding him of the words.

We were sitting in the garden at Graceland. Elvis was wearing a baggy, light blue silk shirt with long collar points and a pair of loose dark blue silk trousers which he thought disguised his weight. I remember the clothes because he nearly always wore jump suits and this outfit was different. I think someone gave him the shirt and the trousers as a Christmas present. We may have been sitting on the porch. We were certainly not sitting inside. The human memory is funny, isn't it? I can't remember precisely where we were sitting but I can remember exactly what Elvis was wearing. He was eating a huge peanut jelly sandwich that looked as if it had been made by cutting a loaf in two and pouring the contents of a jar of jelly in between the two halves. It looked like that because that was what it was. The chefs at Graceland were highly paid, experienced professionals who were probably more accustomed to working with truffles and caviar than with peanut jelly and who could, no doubt, have prepared soufflés and fancy duck dishes if required to do so. Sadly for them, and for Elvis's waistline, they spent most of their time making oversized sandwiches and cooking burgers and hot dogs. I was sipping a diet cola.

I looked at him.

'Just out of interest, tell me how it would work. I'm dead and I move to Paris. Isn't someone going to notice if Elvis Presley suddenly rents a flat and turns up at a nightclub?'

'You wouldn't be Elvis Presley. You'd be someone else.'

'Who? Who am I going to be?'

'I don't know. You'd need a new name. A new passport and a new driving licence. We'd change your appearance so that you didn't look like Elvis Presley.'

'What name? What am I going to call myself?'

'I don't know.'

'I want to be called Jesse Presley.'

'You can't be called Jesse Presley!' I told him, resisting the temptation to laugh. Nothing related to Jesse was a laughing matter.

'Why not?'

'Every Elvis fan knows that Jesse was your twin brother. If Jesse Presley turns up in a hotel register there's going to be a crowd in the lobby before you've unpacked your suitcase.'

Elvis thought about this for a few moments and then nodded. 'So, what's my new name going to be?'

'Elvis, I have no idea! We have to find you a new identity.'

'John Barron. I could be John Barron. I've always liked that name.'

'It doesn't work that way,' I told him. 'Not if you're going to do it properly.'

'I could get someone to make me up some papers as John Barron!' said Elvis. 'I heard of a guy who makes passports and driving licences. You just give him a photo and a name and he makes up the papers.'

'No!' I said. 'If you start off with fake papers you'll always be on the run, always looking over your shoulder, always waiting for someone to spot that something is wrong. And what do you do when those run out? You can't get them renewed because they were never real in the first place.'

'Well, just get someone to ring the President and tell him I want a new passport. I want it in the name of John Barron. He'll do that.'

I explained to him that if we did that then a lot of people would know Elvis Presley's new identity. 'These people are not good at keeping secrets,' I pointed out. 'How long do you think it would be before someone in the White House leaked it that Elvis Presley is alive and well and living in Colorado under the name John Barron.'

'I don't want to go to Colorado! Why would I want to live in Colorado? I don't think I've ever been to Colorado.' He thought for a moment. 'My car has probably been to Colorado. Do you remember that the Colonel once sent my Caddy out on tour?'

'You were in Colorado last year,' I reminded him. 'There were sixteen people with you. Linda Thompson, Joe Exposito and heaven knows who else. You stayed in a hotel in Denver and then rented a big house. You spent your 41st birthday there.'

Elvis laughed. 'I remember that.' He frowned. 'Was that Colorado? I remember I went on the ski slopes at night on one of those motor cycle things with skis. What do they call them?'

'Ski mobiles.'

'I went racing around on one of them ski mobiles and some kid protested that I was breaking the rules. Why would you have rules about something like that?'

'The kid was President Ford's 18 year-old-daughter.'

'Was she?' This made Elvis laugh. 'What happened?' He was laughing so much that his mascara started to run. He often wore mascara in those days.

'You bought Cadillacs and Lincolns for everyone in sight and nothing happened. You even bought a Cadillac for a local TV news reader who reported the fact that you'd bought Cadillacs for everyone in sight.'

'So why am I going to live in Colorado? It sounds like the darned place is full to the brim with Cadillacs already.'

'You're not,' I said gently. 'It was just an illustration. You can't tell anyone your new name. And your passport has to be real – issued by a genuine Passport Office.' I'd learned to be patient. In those days Elvis used to get confused easily. I'm not surprised. Dr Nick had him on so many pills that a rhino would have been confused. When Elvis managed to get off the pills he became a different person; he returned to being the bright, lively individual I'd once known in Paris so many years earlier.

'So how the heck can we get a real passport that's fake?'

'It's not that difficult. It would be best to get hold of British passports. I read about how to do it in a thriller called 'Day of the Jackal'. I go to a cemetery in some little town in England and find the grave of a child who died when he was just two or three years old. I then get hold of a copy of his birth certificate.'

Elvis sat forward, interested. 'How do you do that?'

'I just write to the records office at Somerset House and tell them I lost my birth certificate.'

'And they send you one? No questions?'

'Yes. I pay a dollar or two in English pounds and they send me a new one. I then use that birth certificate to obtain a passport.'

'Is that it?'

'Yes.'

'It's that easy?' Elvis was clearly astonished.

'Pretty much, yes. I fill in a passport application form and send them the birth certificate and a couple of photographs.'

'So I have to go to England to have my picture taken? How do I get to England without anyone knowing?'

'You don't have to go to England. I take a couple of pictures here and we make sure that you don't look too much like Elvis. Glue on a moustache and stick a blond wig on your head. Or we'll put grease on your hair and comb it straight back. Put in a pair of contact lenses. No one ever looks like their passport photo so the picture doesn't matter much. To be doubly sure no one recognises the picture I get the film developed over there in a local chemist. No guy in a chemist shop in England is going to think 'Hey. This is a passport picture of Elvis.' The photographs have to be certified by a doctor or a lawyer or some other such theoretically respectable person but I can just fake that bit. They hardly ever check. I just scribble something on the back of the photos.'

'What if they do check?'

'Then we try again with another name.'

'They won't catch you? Throw you into the Tower of London?'

'No, they won't catch me. I'll send the application from an accommodation address.'

'What's an accommodation address?'

'I pay a shopkeeper a few pounds to have my mail sent to his address.'

'You can do that?'

'Yes.'

Elvis thought about all this for a while. He seemed surprised and impressed. 'So does this mean I have to wear a blond wig and a moustache for ever?'

'No, of course not. People dye their hair and shave off moustaches all the time.'

'You think this could work?'

'Yes. You'd have a genuine passport in a new name. You could start a brand new life as someone else. With a passport you can get everything else you need – bank account, driving licence and social security number, though they call it national insurance number over there. When the passport runs out you just renew it the same way that anyone else renews a passport.'

'Can I be John Barron?'

'No. You have to use the name of the kid who died. You're becoming him.'

'Gee. I've already died once and now I'm being dead again. Don't the people in England who give out passports know I'm dead?'

'No. The people who hand out birth certificates don't have anything to do with the people who store death certificates.'

Elvis thought about this for a moment. 'Is that for real?'

I nodded. 'It's for real. It's a bureaucratic loophole.'

Elvis was quiet again. I could almost hear the cogs clicking over.

'You need to get two passports,' he said at last. 'Can you get two?'

'Yes. I just do the same thing twice in different towns. But why do you need two passports?'

'I don't need two. I need one and you need one.'

'Why do I need one?'

'Because you're coming with me. If I'm going to disappear and die I ain't going by myself. You know Paris. You speak French don't you?'

I hesitated. 'Yes.'

'I can't take Billy with me,' said Elvis. 'He's too well known. If people saw him and me together they'd smell a rat. The same goes for Joe. And I don't want to take a girl. I need someone I can trust. I trust you. I've known you for a long time but hardly anyone knows that. No one much would notice if you disappeared, would they?'

I thought about this for a moment. 'No, I don't suppose they would,' I admitted. It was a chilling thought.

'And it would suit you pretty fine to disappear?'

I nodded. He was right. Starting a new life would solve a lot of problems.

'So what do you say?' He gave me the 1000 watt smile and raised a questioning eyebrow.

Chapter Four

Elvis was right. I did have sound reasons to disappear.

I should point out here that the following few chapters are of interest and consequence only insofar as they explain how and why I came to be the man who helped the world's most famous singing star, show business royalty if ever there was any, to die, disappear and emerge a few months later, unheralded, unrecognised and unknown in another country an ocean away.

I was born in Liverpool, England, and grew up there a good few years before the Beatles and the Cavern nightclub made the city world famous as the new pop music capital of the world. I went to University in Manchester where, for no good reason that I can remember, I studied Modern Languages. After the requisite three years I obtained the piece of paper confirming that I'd lasted the course and was entitled to put the letters B.A. after my name. I then spent five years working my way through two provincial papers (one in Wolverhampton and one in Birmingham) and a national broadsheet. After three years with the broadsheet I managed to be in the right office at the moment when the paper's Paris correspondent phoned in his resignation. `I can do that job,' I told the deputy editor and two days later I found myself moving into a cramped, stuffy and noisy apartment in Montmartre.

I had fifteen glorious months getting to know Paris and then one of those regular economic downturns which the politicians always seem to regard as unexpected and exceptional hit the paper hard and the editor decided that the editorial budget could no longer carry the cost of special correspondents in all the major European cities. The bloke in Berlin got the new job as European Correspondent on the entirely reasonable grounds that he had been with the paper longest and was married to the Finance Director's oldest daughter. The rest of us got a letter of thanks and the statutory goodbye cheque. There were no spare jobs back in London and the paper had even axed its full-time fishing correspondent who had been there since the 1920's and had worked all through the war without getting a single story into the paper. There was a rumour that the editor, the deputy editor and the news editor hadn't even known that the paper had a fishing correspondent.

I decided to stay in Paris, which I was getting to know and like more than any other city I'd worked in (including Wolverhampton) but after three months my goodbye money was beginning to run out and the failure of an ardent letter writing campaign made it abundantly clear that no British or American papers were looking for a Paris correspondent. I wrote a few articles as a freelance but although the payments for these helped pay my bar bills I needed something more substantial and more reliable to pay the rent and to buy dull necessities such as food, clothing and cigarettes.

That was when I found an unlikely fairy godmother in the guise of the manager of a night club on the Champs Élysées.

Innocent Fabian, the manager, was the wife of the club's owner, Sebastien, but after years of over-indulgence, and three strokes, Sebastien, by now in his eighties, had been forced into what he considered to be early retirement. He hardly ever budged from their luxurious fifth floor apartment in an 18th century building on the Isle de la Citie and spent his days watching boats chugging up and down the Seine. Occasionally, tourists would see him staring down at them and they would wave. He never waved back. Innocent, who looked to be in her early fifties in the daylight and her forties in the dimly lit club, was actually only fifteen years younger than her husband.

In those days, the big, well-known clubs in Paris were far more decent than their reputations suggested and the club owned by the Fabians catered largely to visiting businessmen who surprisingly often took along their wives to see the shows. `My girls are all virgins when they start work,' Innocent once boasted. `And they are all still virgins when they retire.' Most of the girls ended up marrying the richest of the businessmen who frequented the club and Innocent boasted that the club's alumnae included more millionairesses than Yale and Harvard combined. She was probably right.

I had been to the Fabian's club no more than half a dozen times but I knew Innocent because I had once written a feature about three English showgirls who worked there. One girl was the daughter of a vicar, one the daughter of an ophthalmologist and the third the daughter of a retired general. Accompanied by a picture of the girls in their glittery costumes and feathery headdresses it made a good story. Walking down the Champs Élysées one day it occurred to me that I might be able to sell a follow up story to the same paper or a story with a different angle to another paper. If I could find three girls from Australia or, better still, from America, I could perhaps sell similar stories to papers in those countries.

It was three in the afternoon and the club was closed to customers but by showing my press card I managed to persuade one of the doormen to let me in. I found Innocent watching rehearsals for a new dance routine. She was wearing a sparkly dark blue evening dress which looked expensive and undoubtedly was and had an opened bottle of Dom Perignon in an ice bucket and a half full glass on a table in front of her. She liked everyone in the club to wear evening dress even during the daytime. Even her secretary and the people in the accounts office wore evening dress. Only the cleaners, who came in very early in the morning and who were, for some reason, exclusively Algerian, were exempt from this rule.

Sadly, my idea for franchising my article on foreign-born dancers fell flat when it turned out that all the girls currently working at the club were as home grown as Champagne and Brie. Even the three English girls had left. The vicar's daughter had gone back home after Daddy found out that she wasn't working as a secretary at the British Embassy as had previously been advertised. The doctor's daughter had taken a job at the Folies Bergere because it was nearer to her flat. And the general's daughter had married a newspaper magnate from Arizona and was now expecting her first child. Innocent tried to keep up with the lives of her former girls and had a filing cabinet drawer full of letters and photographs.

'Why don't you come and work for me,' said Innocent. She'd sensed my desperation and disappointment when the story idea had collapsed and I had explained that I'd lost my job with the paper and was now freelancing.

I looked at her and nearly dropped the glass I was holding. (She'd called for a spare glass as soon as she'd seen me arrive.)

'What on earth can I do for you?' I asked. 'I've got no boobs, I can't dance and I'd make a terrible waiter.'

'You could be the club's press agent,' she said simply. 'We have never had one. But some of the new clubs have hired agents and they are now getting all the publicity. You could think up ways to get stories in the papers. And when we have celebrities in the club you could tip off the photographers so that they could take pictures.'

And so we shook hands on a deal there and then. Innocent offered to pay me almost twice what the paper had been paying me and gave me enough of an advance to pay for a new dinner suit, a few dress shirts and a bow tie. It wasn't exactly what I'd dreamt of doing when I'd decided I wanted to be a journalist but it was a damned sight better than court reporting in Wolverhampton.

Chapter Five

I don't know how or why Elvis chose to visit the club but I could hardly believe my eyes when he and a bunch of army mates wandered in one Saturday evening. There was no advance notice and they made no fuss. Apart from the fact that one of them was the biggest music star the world had ever seen they could have been just a group of army guys enjoying a weekend furlough. I'd been working there for about three months and the club had enjoyed visits from the usual French celebrities throughout that time. Innocent used to give them free champagne if they were famous enough to be ogled by the other customers. French rock star Johnny Hallyday was a regular visitor. Innocent used to park one of the doormen (we didn't call them bouncers) by their table so that they weren't bothered by autograph hunters. Most American movie stars who came to Paris tried to get photographed in one club or another (I think they felt that being pictured in a famous Parisian night spot gave them a sophisticated sheen) and I suppose we had our fair share of the international stars. I seem to remember playing host to Vincent Price, Peter O'Toole and Audrey Hepburn. Lots of movie directors came too, but no one recognised them and Innocent never bothered to send them the free champagne.

Elvis was different.

He was the only celebrity I ever met who wasn't particularly keen on being photographed or interviewed and we quickly realised that he was such a huge star that we couldn't treat him like the others. The problem was that as soon as it became known that the King was in the club a huge crowd would develop in the street outside. This was a bad thing because it meant that paying customers couldn't get to the door and simply told their driver to take them to another club. Innocent and I talked with Elvis and we agreed that when he wanted to come to the club he would arrive at the back door and enter through the kitchens. Once inside the club it was fairly easy to control any publicity. Press photographers could either be kept out of the area where Elvis was sitting or excluded from the club completely. And since there were no mobile phones in those days, and no public call boxes within the club, it was pretty well impossible for anyone who saw him to spread the word to friends outside. The result was that Elvis could enjoy a fairly peaceful night out without the club's takings being damaged. The girls who worked in the club were, not surprisingly, desperate to be invited to his table. Innocent once admitted to me that by the time Elvis's stay in Germany came to an end, and his visits to the club finished, she was confident that there wasn't a single virgin working in the club. The King of Rock and Roll had personally deflowered every single one of them. During one week long stay he became dangerously close to going to bed with a beautiful and convincing transsexual called April Ashley who worked as a dancer in the club. When I took him aside and asked him if he knew exactly what he was getting into he went bright red with embarrassment. He was, however, enough of a gentleman to send 'her' a bottle of champagne every night for the remainder of that stay in Paris.

I got on well with Elvis and gradually came to know him as a friend. He was naturally nervous with strangers but years of being chased by fans and surrounded by hangers-on had left him desperately lonely and keen to grow friendships with people he felt he could trust. He knew that there were many stories about him that I could have easily sold to the press ('Elvis Deflowers Three Virgins In One Steamy Night' would have earned me a year's salary) but also knew that I had kept these tales to myself.

'I trust you as much as I've ever trusted anyone,' he said, when he left Paris for the last time. 'Come back to the States with me. You can be my press agent. Tour with me. Look after me. Deal with the journalists. You know how these things work.' He offered me an absurdly large salary and doubled it when I thanked him but said 'No'. I had hooked up with Jonquil, a girl who danced at Le Moulin Rouge and she wouldn't leave Paris. I thought I was in love and I thought she was in love too. We talked of ditching our two small apartments and renting one big one. We talked of a wedding and babies. When I told Elvis why I wasn't leaving he offered to get her a job in Las Vegas. But she wouldn't budge. She wanted to stay in Paris. And so I said 'No' to Elvis and stayed with Jonquil and spent my Saturdays walking around La Samaritaine and looking at soft furnishings and my Sundays looking at two and three bedroom apartments. 'I won't forget you,' said Elvis, when he left Paris for the last time. 'If you ever need anything come and see me.' He smiled and gripped my arm. 'Come and see me anyway. Come and stay.' I promised that I would. He told me that in 1957 he'd given his parents a budget of $100,000 to buy him a house big enough and private enough for the family and the growing Presley entourage. They had bought him a Colonial style mansion called Graceland.

    I stayed at the club for nine months after Elvis went back to the States but although it certainly wasn't a bad life it wasn't a particularly rewarding one. I was well paid to drink champagne and eat excellent food with celebrities and beautiful, scantily clad women and for many people that would have been more than enough. But then Jonquil suddenly announced that she was leaving me and it turned out that although she was in love she was not in love with me. She had been having an affair with a Brazilian millionaire and he had invited her to go to Brazil with him. He had a Ferrari, a huge mansion in Rio de Janeiro, a yacht moored permanently in Cannes and a divorce lawyer who was disposing of his wife for him.

    I was devastated. It seemed as if the world had ended. I moped around for a week or two and then decided that I had to leave Paris. I had no friends and no ties and I needed go get away. Moreover, I was still young enough to want to find a little adventure in life. I wanted to travel a little more. I wanted to stretch myself and see what I could do. I was young enough, cocky enough and inexperienced enough to think that the world was my oyster and that all I needed was to find a way to grab the pearl that was sitting there waiting for me.

    I gave Innocent a month's notice, sold the meagre collection of furniture in my apartment and bought a plane ticket to Los Angeles. I had a film script I'd half-finished and I thought I'd try to sell it in Hollywood.

Chapter Six

I travelled to America without mishap and finished my screenplay without too much difficulty. But after that things went wrong with such monotonous regularity that I began to wonder if I had accidentally broken a mirror while living in Paris.

My first problem was that I couldn't find an agent prepared to handle my script. I tried 27 and they were all too important, too busy or too rude to give me an appointment or to read the damned thing. I eventually managed to find a young producer who was prepared to read it. He scribbled notes all over it (meaning that I would have to retype it all before offering it to anyone else) and told me that it would be far too expensive for anyone other than a major studio. An actress I met (who was so successful in her chosen industry that she was working as a waitress at the time) told me that the script stank because there weren't enough parts in it for women. In the end, in despair, I threw the only copy I had into a dumpster and spent my last dollars on a plane ticket back to London. I'd heard that things had picked up in England and that my old paper was hiring journalists again. I hoped they might give me a job.

Two weeks later I was working as a general news reporter, covering everything from disasters to funerals, and weddings to strikes. They were busy days and although I remembered my days in Paris with great fondness they seemed to have taken place a lifetime ago. I tried not to think of them too much because I didn't want to be one of those sad guys who live their lives as though in a rowing boat; slowly moving onwards while forever looking behind at where they've been. But it was difficult to forget those days with Elvis, Innocent and Jonquil. I still thought of Jonquil more often than was good for me. Occasionally, I saw photographs of her and her husband welcoming film stars to their yacht or attending first night parties. I did not think they seemed to be a happy couple. I still hadn't married, though there had been one or two near misses. My peculiar working hours didn't help. I ate far too much fast food, put on weight and acquired the inevitable newspaperman's ulcer.

As the years wandered by I gradually moved up the editorial ladder and eventually reached the heady heights of assistant news editor. I did everything at the paper from making up weather forecasts (when the official forecasts didn't turn up) to writing the astrology column (when the paper's astrologer had an unforeseen accident and broke a wrist).

Every Christmas I would promise myself that I'd leave and try something else. I felt strangely unsatisfied but if anyone had asked me why I felt unfulfilled I would not have been able to explain; I honestly didn't know what else I should be doing with my life. And then, in 1976, I decided that I had to make a move. I had written a novel that had been published and I thought I was going to be a great success at last. I resigned from the newspaper and flew to America. I have no idea why but I had decided that if I was going to be a successful novelist I had to write something more in tune with the needs of American readers. It was a silly thing to do and everything went wrong. A wiser man would have doubtless learnt something from his first trans-Atlantic misadventure. My publishers rejected my second novel and so did every other publisher I sent it to. My first novel had received surprisingly encouraging reviews but the sales had been so bad that the book hadn't earned enough to pay its advance. I was not, it seemed, destined to find riches from America's paperback industry.

When my savings ran out I found myself living in a strange country with no means of supporting myself. I cannot now remember why I was there but I found myself in Chicago and after a number of humiliating interviews with hard-nosed news editors who needed a limey journalist as much as they needed another bout of heartburn I eventually managed to get myself a job on a weekly magazine which had a readership small enough to fit into one of those miniature theatres which exist off, off, off Broadway. My job was to find would-be celebrities who wanted to be profiled but who could bring in advertising revenue. After three weeks interviewing local restaurant owners, architects and real estate operatives I was seduced (I'm sorry but there is no other word for it) by a woman who called herself an interior decorator and boasted that she was the woman who had introduced bed cushions to the meat-packing centre of the United States of America. I wrote the interview with her, the magazine published it and the whole sordid deal was paid for with half a dozen quarter page advertisements. We had a brief but torrid affair before I discovered that she was married and that her husband was not the sort of person who was willing to be cuckolded by a woefully unsuccessful English journalist or, I suspect, anyone else who couldn't deliver a solid block of votes at the next election. He was something big in local politics and had pudgy fingers in enough pies to feed an army. Two goons in expensive suits visited me at the hotel where I was staying and suggested that I might give serious consideration to leaving town. When I explained that I was broke and had to wait for my pay cheque one of them stuffed a $100 bill into my shirt pocket and they gave me a ride to the bus station. They assured me, very politely, that if I was still around the following day I would be provided with an unprecedented opportunity to assess the inadequacies of American health care at the lower end of the market.

'The boss told us to break your legs just for fun,' said one of the goons, when I'd bought my ticket. 'Or your arms. He gave us the choice. He gives us a certain amount of discretion in these things.'

'But it ain't your fault,' said the other. 'The truth is that his wife will screw anything in trousers. You ain't nothing special. It don't seem right to keep breaking guys' legs just because his wife is a nympho who can't keep her knickers on.' I didn't think it appropriate to mention that if my experience was reliable she never wore any.

'Which ain't to say we won't break a few bones if we see you again,' said the first, in case I thought they'd gone soft.

'Might be best for you to keep a low profile,' said the second. 'Hide away for a few years. If the boss finds you're still around, and he's in a bad mood, he's likely to get irritated.'

I headed for Memphis, Tennessee and Graceland.

Chapter Seven

When I arrived at the mansion, Elvis treated me like a long lost brother. He hired me as a press agent and gave me a room at Graceland. I hardly recognised him. I'd seen pictures, of course, but they hadn't prepared me for the bloating and the colour of his skin. He looked as if he ought to be in hospital. If someone had told me he was dying I would have believed them. His doctor, a Greek physician known simply as Dr Nick (whom I grew to despise), wrote out prescriptions as though afraid that the ink in his pen would dry up if he didn't keep scribbling. Elvis's pill collection would have filled the shelves of any small town pharmacy.

Elvis would not have minded if I had spent my days lounging around Graceland, doing as little as the many regular hangers on, but I've always liked to feel that I'm earning my keep and so I did what I could for the man and the image (which were not always the same thing).

I soon found that instead of just trying to get publicity for Elvis I would need to spend most of my time attempting to manage the publicity he was going to get anyway. I once read that the Queen of England's press secretary had said that his job was not to get his employer into the press but to keep her out of it and I soon understood what he meant. Elvis's huge success meant that there were too many journalists and music critics who enjoyed jumping up and down on his reputation now that he was overweight and out of condition. It didn't seem to occur to any of them that there was a direct link between their nastiness and Elvis's physical condition. I really don't think any of them understood just how sensitive Elvis could be to criticism, or that it was as a response to the criticism that he took drugs and ate too much. The saddest thing was that the nastiest critics worked either in America or Britain. Writers in other parts of the world, particularly Asia and mainland Europe, still remained loyal subjects.

Among other things I did I found myself helping to organise, or, at least, overseeing, some of the biggest 'Elvis Lookalike' competitions. These were already hugely popular and to my astonishment I discovered that the first Elvis impersonator had appeared back in the mid 1950s when Elvis's career had only just started. Today, of course, there are vast numbers of professional Elvis impersonators (usually known as `tribute acts) and I've heard that there are even radio stations which do nothing else but broadcast material recorded by Elvis impersonators.

Elvis lookalike competitions had really become popular in the early 1970's when a singer called Phil Ochs appeared at the Carnegie Hall wearing an Elvis-style gold lame suit which looked just like the real thing. This was not surprising since it had been made for him by Nudie Cohen; the costumier who made Elvis's stage clothes. And then, in the mid 1970's, an actor called Andy Kaufman made an Elvis impersonation part of his act. Elvis once told me that he thought Kaufman was the best impersonator of them all. People may find this difficult to believe but the Colonel and several members of the Memphis Mafia once spent several hours wondering if they could hire Kaufman to perform Elvis's shows for him. It was the Colonel himself who eventually decided that the risk was too great. But they did think about it for quite a while, though when I later talked to Elvis about it he said that no one had ever mentioned the idea to him. He was amused rather than annoyed by it.

My responsibility was to try to make sure that the worst and most comical impersonators were weeded out at a very early stage. I didn't want really fat men in absurd costumes and bad wigs stumbling around on the stage and forgetting their words.

It was while I was engaged in helping to edit out some of the worst performances for a televised Elvis lookalike competition that I met a man called Donald Case.

Case was a 43-year-old former Walmart employee who had retired early through ill health and who was now trying to supplement his disability pension by impersonating Elvis. He had a weak heart but most of his health problems were caused by the fact that he was grossly overweight. As an Elvis impersonator he had a couple of major disadvantages: he couldn't sing at all and he was in such poor condition that he had to be helped on and off the stage and certainly couldn't do any hip waving while he was out there. When he opened his mouth the sound that came out of it was unique. When he was tackling the higher notes he sounded just like a misfiring chain saw and when he moved onto the lower notes he sounded like a flushing toilet. But he had one enormous advantage: he looked just like Elvis. I don't mean he looked a bit like Elvis. He was the spitting image of Elvis. He had the hair, the eyes, the nose and even, unbelievably, the mouth. He was pretty much the same height and he must have measured pretty much the same around the waist too. I once asked him why he didn't try to lose a little weight. He told me that if he lost weight he wouldn't look like Elvis and that he'd rather die than not look like the King. He had a stage costume made out of some variety of nylon. He wore it all the time, even when shopping or travelling by bus. Originally, the chest and shoulders had been decorated with rhinestones but, with all the travelling, some of these had been lost. When I took some photographs of Donald and showed them to people back at Graceland no one could tell that they weren't photographs of Elvis himself. Even Elvis couldn't believe they were photographs of someone else. Some of the crew who lived with Elvis sneered at impersonators but Elvis never sneered. He admired and respected them. To him they were the `superfans'. If judges had picked a winner on appearances alone Donald would have won every competition he entered. Sadly, his appalling singing and inability to move more than the smallest of muscles without gasping for breath meant that the best he ever managed was a third place in a competition in Idaho. I really should have excluded him from the competitions but I liked him too much to wreck his dream. And he did look just like Elvis.

    I liked Donald (he was always Donald and never Don) and spent some time talking to him and getting to know him. His enthusiasm and passion for Elvis was honest, uncomplicated and unquestioning. He was overjoyed when I gave him a signed photograph, a scarf and some other Elvis memorabilia. I even gave him a letter from Elvis telling him that he was the best `lookalike' in the business and that if Elvis ever made any more movies he, Donald, would be hired as the stand in. He had the letter framed and kept it, together with his other few possessions, in a storage locker in Memphis which was the nearest place he had to a home.

    Donald was a lonely man. He had never married, he had no siblings and his parents had both died early of heart disease. He told me he knew he did not have long on this earth. Doctors told him he needed heart bypass surgery. `I wouldn't have it even if I could afford it,' he said. `I hate hospitals. I'd rather die than have an operation. He told me that every time he went on stage he suffered chest pains. `I'd love to die impersonating Elvis,' he said.

He spent his days wandering around the country entering (but never winning) Elvis Presley competitions. He lived in cheap motels where, if you were lucky, the management changed the bed sheets one at a time and vacuumed the floors once a month. One a week he washed out his white, tasselled stage suit in the bathroom sink and hung it on the shower curtain rail to dry overnight.

I attended a couple of the competitions Donald entered and found them curious affairs. The contestants I saw could be divided into two groups: the ones who could sing and dance a bit but who, despite growing their sideburns and spending a small fortune on hair lacquer, didn't look anything like Elvis and the ones who wouldn't have been able to sing a note if you'd stood them on a hotplate and offered them a fat recording contract, but who looked like Elvis. Some looked like him as he had been in the late 1950s or early 1960s. But most, like Donald, looked like the later, larger model. The vast majority of the impersonators were men, of course, but I did meet a couple of women who entered the competitions. And a surprising number of Orientals who used Sellotape and stage glue to try and reshape their eyes.

I used to try hard to persuade the promoters to exclude the ones who weren't taking the thing reasonably seriously. I remember we had a lot of trouble with a 55-year-old woman who wanted to enter. She was under five feet tall but weighed over 200 pounds and I reckon half of that must have been down to her boobs. You could never tell what she was going to do. Once she taped her breasts flat and did it so tightly that she fainted and landed in the middle of the orchestra. On another occasion she went on stage topless and nearly caused a riot. I eventually managed to get rid of her by suggesting she entered Dolly Parton lookalike competitions. She was delighted by this idea, which had apparently never crossed her mind, and I later read that with the aid of an enormous, daffodil yellow wig and the support of a custom made bra she had become a regular winner on the Dolly Parton Lookalike circuit. There can be no doubting that America is a wonderful country with opportunities for everyone.

Chapter Eight

'So, what do you say?' asked Elvis, for a second time. We were still sitting in the garden and neither of us had spoken for a while.

'There aren't many people who know that we know each other, but there are a few. If we're going to do this properly we both have to die and we both have to start again, with new names and new identities.' I was by now past the age of personal ambition but it was clear to me that this was the greatest chance I would ever have for an adventure on an epic scale. Besides, I liked Elvis very much. In Paris I had grown close to the shy, modest and surprisingly sensitive young soldier with the prodigious talent for entertaining people, and now I wanted to help him. The Elvis I saw beside me was obese, desperate and care ridden. It was difficult to believe that the young man with the world laid before him had grown into this sad pastiche; so very different to the boy in his 20s whom I had known in Paris.

'Do you want to do it?'

'I haven't got any reason not to,' I told him. 'My first attempt at life hasn't been too successful.' It seemed ironic. He needed to die because his life had been too successful and I was happy to die because mine had been a failure. I paused and then told him about my romance with the interior designer in Chicago and the ensuing difficulties with her well-connected husband. Elvis thought this was very funny.

'It sounds like you've got a good reason to get out of America,' he said. 'But I could just get someone to have a word with the husband.' Elvis always believed that he could solve people's problems simply by using his name. And most of the time he was right. If someone from Graceland had rung Chicago I suspect that the husband who had sent his goons to break my legs would have probably offered to lend me his wife on weekends and bank holidays.

'With me it's more that I haven't got a good reason to stay,' I told him. 'And I rather like the idea of starting again without history, without baggage. A fresh start.' It seemed like an adventure I couldn't refuse. I had the advantage of not having any relatives to worry about. And my life wasn't exactly overflowing with friends either.

'So, what do you say? Are you on for this? Shall we do it?'

I looked at him. 'Are you really serious about this? You're prepared to give up being Elvis Presley? Prepared to walk away from Graceland? Prepared to abandon the fans, the adulation and the money? Prepared never to see again the people you love and know?'

The odd thing was that I wasn't at all sure that I wanted to get involved. Part of me was certain that if I helped Elvis escape from his life I might grow to regret it. He had been pampered for so long that in some ways looking after him would, to begin with at least, be like looking after a child or an invalid. But part of me was aware that if he chose to escape and I didn't go with him I would regret the missed opportunity for the rest of my life.

There was a long, long silence.

'I don't know who loves me anymore,' he said. 'I don't know who to trust. I don't want to leave Lisa Marie but she'll be better off without me. She can grow up without kids at school laughing at her daddy. No one bothers to laugh at dead people.'

'She'll always love you,' I told him. I glanced across. There were tears in his eyes. Suddenly, I knew that for me that the regret of doing nothing would be infinitely greater than the regret of going with him.

'I used to trust the Colonel,' said Elvis. 'Without him I wouldn't be Elvis Presley. I know that. But he's got mean and greedy.' I'd never heard him talk about the Colonel that way before and I don't think anyone else ever did. 'I have to do these shows because he owes people,' said Elvis. 'I can't let him down because they want their money.' I don't think anyone, especially the Colonel, realised that Elvis knew why he was being railroaded into concerts he didn't want to do.

'If you die there will be plenty of money,' I told him.

'I know that,' he said. 'Record sales will go through the roof.' He smiled and twitched the lip. 'I'll have a string of top ten hits again.' He frowned slightly. 'It's strange to think that I'll be more successful dead than I am alive.'

'Audiences are fickle,' I said. 'And we often only really appreciate people when they're gone.'

'I guess that's so,' said Elvis thoughtfully.

'We have to talk to the Colonel.'.

'You have to talk to the Colonel,' said Elvis, putting the emphasis on the first word. 'And to Vernon. Both of them. I want them to know. Besides, we'll need some money won't we?'

'We will,' I agreed.

'Have you got any?'

I took out my wallet. 'I've got 73 dollars.'

'That's not going to get us out of Memphis.'

'No.'

'I've got less than you. I ain't got a dollar.'

I looked at him. Elvis Presley. The most successful entertainer in the history of the world. Could he really be broke?

'It's the expenses,' said Elvis. 'I get 50% of what I earn but it just disappears. The Colonel is always telling me I'm broke.'

I looked at him. 'What happens to the other 50%?'

'That's for the Colonel.'

'The Colonel takes 50% of what you earn?' I knew that the Colonel took a huge percentage of Elvis's earnings but I hadn't known that he was taking half.

'Without him I wouldn't be who I am. He made me a star.' Elvis sounded defensive as he often did when talking about the Colonel. The two men had a strange relationship. Half respect and half fear on Elvis's side and half respect and half contempt on the Colonel's side. I sometimes thought that the Colonel treated Elvis the same way that an organ grinder treated his monkey.

'Even so…half of your earnings seems rather a lot.'

'And I have big expenses out of my half. And taxes.

'You'll have to stop giving away Cadillacs,' I told him. 'You've given away 46 Cadillacs so far this year. Perhaps try cutting down slowly. Just give away a few Fords. Then a few of those foreign compacts. And get yourself down to a couple of bicycles every six months.'

Elvis laughed.

'Shouldn't you tell them?' I asked him.

'I'll get myself all mixed up,' said Elvis. 'You'll explain things better than I could.' There were tears in his eyes. I thought the tears were there because talking of death had reminded him of his mother. He always cried when he talked or thought about her. But it wasn't that at all. 'Do you think I'm losing my mind?' he asked. 'I sometimes think I'm losing my darned mind. I can't remember stuff. I can't think clearly.'

'It's just the pills you're taking,' I told him. 'We have to get off you them.'

'Dr Nick says he's tried to get me off the pills,' said Elvis.

'Maybe. But you started taking the drugs partly because you were worrying about the prospect of the new shows and partly because you were upset by all the criticism. And none of that has changed.'

'That book ain't been a help,' said Elvis. 'I could shoot that ungrateful pair.' He took a gun out from underneath his shirt and pointed it at a tree.

'They'd deserve it,' I told him. 'But, unfortunately I don't think it's open season on authors just yet.'

'I could make us some money by doing concerts. Maybe signing some pictures.'

'You can't ever do a concert again,' I told him. 'If you step on a stage every member of the audience will know Elvis is alive. And you can't sign photographs – or anything else.'

He thought for a while. 'No. I guess not.'

'Besides, you told me you didn't want to do any more concerts.'

'I don't. But we'll need some money. Plane tickets. Hotels. Buying those passports. All that stuff.'

'And to live on.'

'Yeah. Food and things like that.'

'Money for food is always good.'

'You think I'll be able to manage without the drugs when I'm dead?'

'Definitely!'

'And maybe I can get rid of some of this flab?' He tapped his abdomen in disgust. 'I hate all this blubber.'

'You'll be off the pills and sixty pounds lighter by Christmas,' I told him.

He looked at me, wanting to believe.

'You'll be off the pills and sixty pounds lighter,' I repeated. I was beginning to think that Elvis was braver and more prepared to be daring than I had suspected.

'You'll tell the Colonel?' he asked.

'I'll tell the Colonel.'

'Tell him first. Then tell my daddy after you've told the Colonel.'
'OK.'

Elvis thought for a while. I waited for him to change his mind.
'No. You'd better tell them both together.'

'OK.'

'There is one other thing that's occurred to me.'

'What's that?'

'If I'm going to die I'll have to be buried and if I'm going to be buried there'll have to be a gravestone won't there? Some sort of memorial stone?'

'I expect there will,' I said. 'Of course there will.'

'I don't want my name on it,' said Elvis. 'That would be spooky. Knowing that there was a gravestone sitting there with my name on it.'

'I think there would have to be a gravestone, Elvis,' I said. 'The fans would expect one. The Colonel would want to give them what they wanted.'

'I'm not happy about that,' said Elvis. 'I understand that the fans would want it but I don't think it would be right.'

We sat in silence for a while. All we could hear was the wind rustling leaves in the trees.

'Maybe they could misspell my name,' suggested Elvis. 'So that I'd know it wasn't really me. So I wouldn't feel like I really had died.' He twirled his gun around, like a gunfighter showing off.

'I think people would notice,' I said. 'There aren't many ways to spell Elvis and I think the fans would notice if they spelt Presley with an extra S or missed the Y off the end.'

'I guess so.'

'Your middle name,' I said suddenly. 'Aaron.'

'Damned silly name. I never did like that name. I never said so because I didn't want to upset my mummy and daddy. But why did they give me a name like that?'

'They could misspell that,' I said. 'Miss out an A and make it Aron. Most people wouldn't notice. And those who did would just blame the stone mason.'

'We could do that,' said Elvis. He turned and smiled. 'Yes. I like that.' He punched me playfully on the arm. 'When we're old and grey and you write the book about how you faked Elvis Presley's death you can put that in there. How we misspelt my middle name so that I never really died. Elvis never really died at all. He lives on.'

I nodded. I honestly couldn't imagine myself ever writing a book about faking Elvis's death. I was even beginning to wonder if we really could get away with it. I still had no idea how we could arrange Elvis's death but I knew that we would need some help. And we'd need a fake body. I was confident that I could find a way to create a new identity for Elvis. I was pretty sure I could think of a way to get him out of the country. But we had to tell someone because we would have to make sure that in the inevitable chaos and consternation no one questioned whether Elvis really was dead. And we would need money. The Colonel and Vernon Presley were the only two people we could trust with the truth. They both needed the money that Elvis's estate would bring in after his death and I was confident they wouldn't say or do anything to jeopardise the flow of cash which we all knew would follow Elvis's tragic and untimely demise. And the money Elvis and I would need would have to come from the Colonel.

Suddenly, there was a bang and Elvis shot the tree.

Well, actually, he shot at the tree. He didn't actually hit it.

Chapter Nine

The Colonel and Elvis's father were surprisingly enthusiastic when I told them that Elvis was going to die. At first they showed some reservations but those disappeared when they understood that Elvis wasn't going to die for real. They both seemed relieved that he wasn't going to commit suicide and I wasn't going to shoot him.

'You mean he's just going to pretend to die?' asked the Colonel who didn't always catch on quite as quickly as his reputation suggested he might. He was wearing a blue linen jacket, a white shirt with the collar folded out over the jacket collar, and a pair of dark grey trousers. He had a cigar clamped between his teeth. The cigar had gone out some time ago.

'That's right.'

'Better than suicide,' said the Colonel, with a firm nod. 'Suicide would be a bad career move.' He thought for a few moments. Although he sometimes seemed to be rather slow and half-witted he had a mind as sharp as a razor where deals were concerned. 'We've got concerts fixed for Las Vegas. He has to do the concerts first,' said the Colonel, who seemed worried. These were the concerts the Colonel had fixed up to help pay off his huge gambling debts. They were the concerts that Elvis didn't want to do. They were one of the major reasons why Elvis wanted to disappear.

'He needs to go before then,' I said.

'Dying could be a good career move,' said the Colonel ignoring me. He had belatedly realised that he could make far more money out of a dead Elvis than out of a live one. 'We'll do a boxed set of albums celebrating his life. Release old concert footage.' His brain was now running at full speed. He took the cigar out of his mouth and waved it around. 'You'll need a body,' he said. 'There will have to be a body. Folk won't accept Elvis is dead if there isn't a body.'

'I know,' I said. 'And it'll have to be something pretty convincing – though we're going to rely heavily on you and Vernon identifying the body as Elvis.'

'Wax would be good,' said the Colonel.

'Won't there have to be a doctor to certify the death?' asked Vernon. 'A coroner or suchlike?'

'We know a few people in the coroner's department,' said the Colonel quickly. 'I can buy a signature with a box of T-shirts. They'll certify a wax dummy if we tell them to.'

I shook my head. 'No bribes,' I said quickly. 'No one else can know. Everyone has to believe that Elvis really is dead. Even the coroner has to believe that Elvis is dead. He has to believe that the body he's certified is Elvis Aaron Presley.'

'How in darnation are you going to do that, boy?' demanded the Colonel. 'That'll be some trick if you can pull it off.' He thought for a moment and then waved the cigar around. Ash fell on his jacket and trousers but he didn't notice. When he was contemplating a deal or a scam he wouldn't notice if he caught fire. 'You going to use some of that Eastern mystical mumbo jumbo? Make my boy look like he's dead when he's really just asleep? Slow his heart right down through meditation? That what you going to do? You could use drugs instead of meditation. They make drugs that will do that. Dr Nick could get us something.'

'It's a good idea,' I agreed. 'But we can't tell Dr Nick.'

'No, I guess not,' said the Colonel. He looked at me. 'You sort it out. That's your responsibility. That's what we're paying you for.'

I didn't remember seeing anything in my employment contract about faking Elvis's death. But I didn't say anything. To be honest I didn't want either the Colonel or Vernon taking too much of a part in the planning of Elvis's death. If the Colonel planned it there would be a chorus of dancing girls on the sidelines and heavenly backing music played by a sixty piece string orchestra. The Colonel wasn't into subtlety. And if Vernon planned it we'd probably all be arrested.

'What'll happen to Graceland?' asked Vernon. He was wearing a plaid shirt and a pair of jeans. I noticed that he had spilt jam down the front of the shirt.

'I've no idea,' I said. 'You could turn it into a museum.'

'That would be fine,' said Vernon, nodding cautiously.

'We could arrange tours,' said the Colonel, who'd been listening as well as scheming. 'Like they have tours of the White House and those palaces in England. Charge ten dollars for a tour of the house and gardens. Have a shop at the end of the tour. Sell photographs, videos, albums, little figurines of Elvis.'

'And the house on Dolan Drive?' asked Vernon.

'Tea towels with pictures of Elvis on them. Cigarette lighters with Elvis on 'em. Christmas tree decorations. Those little cork mats people use to put their drinks on so that they don't damage the varnish on their table. What do they call those damned things?'

'Coasters,' I told the Colonel. 'I'm sure Elvis will want you to carry on living there,' I said to Vernon. 'Or I suppose you and Dee could move back into Graceland.' Elvis had disapproved of his father's second marriage and had eventually thrown his daddy and Dee, his daddy's second wife, out of Graceland and had bought them a house on Dolan Drive bordering the Graceland estate.

They both seemed contented. True to form, their concern had only been for themselves – and the money they might be able to make.

'We could set up a company to organise the tours and the memorial memorabilia,' said Vernon.

'Sell the rights,' insisted the Colonel. 'Let someone else do the worrying. We just charge them fees, big fees.'

'You ain't taking half of this,' said Vernon. 'Not the memorabilia.'

'We'll sort something out,' said the Colonel reaching out and patting him on the arm. 'No need for us to fall out over something like money.'

Vernon mumbled something which I didn't catch. I'd only known the Colonel for a short time but I could hardly believe what I'd heard. I couldn't imagine the Colonel falling out with anyone over anything other than money.

'If he dies it'll have to be permanent,' said the Colonel to me. 'No come backs. No more records. No more tours.' He stared at me and stabbed the cigar in my direction. 'Permanent,' he said. 'Does my boy know that?' I nodded. The Colonel thought for a moment. 'I suppose we could record a few more tracks to release after he dies.'

'You've already got more than enough stuff to release' I told him. They had both annoyed me. They were both clearly excited by how they would benefit when Elvis 'died'. I couldn't help noticing that neither the Colonel nor Vernon had asked where Elvis would go or what he would do with the rest of his life. (I did not tell Elvis any of this until they had both died, a few years later. I told him then because I knew it would make their passing much easier for him.

Subsequent events showed that he did not owe either of them a single tear.)

'You can't tell anyone,' I told them both. 'Only the four of us will know. If word gets out that Elvis is still alive you two will probably end up in prison and the money supermarket will close for good.'

They both thought about this. Neither of them fancied the idea of prison. For Vernon it would be a return engagement. And neither of them was keen on the idea of having to make an ordinary living without Elvis.

'Four people?' said Vernon suddenly He looked around and mentally counted up to three. It was clearly an effort which strained his skills to the limit. 'There's only three of us here.'

'We'll have to tell Elvis,' I said dryly. 'He's the fourth.'

'Oh, sure,' said Vernon, nodding. If he'd been a brain surgeon not many of his patients would have survived.

'None of us can tell anyone else,' I repeated. I looked at Vernon. 'You can't tell Dee. Even on your deathbed you can't tell anyone.'

'Hell I can keep a secret,' said Vernon. I heard him but I wasn't really listening. It had belatedly occurred to me that five people, not four, had to be in on the secret; though we would not have to worry about the fifth keeping his mouth shut because the fifth would not be alive to talk. And I thought I knew who the fifth man would be. I could still remember him saying: 'I want to die impersonating Elvis.'

'We'll need some money,' I told the Colonel. 'To cover our immediate expenses. And Elvis will need money to live on. It won't be easy for him to get a job.'

The Colonel pulled a face.

' It's a long time since he drove a truck,' I pointed out.

'How much do you want?' he asked. 'For yourself?'

'I don't want anything for myself. I'll earn my own living. But you have to give Elvis some money. You owe him that.'

'There isn't any money,' said the Colonel immediately. It was a reflex action.

'The money has all gone on salaries and Cadillacs and gifts to people he didn't even half know,' said Vernon bitterly. He had never found it easy to accept Elvis's generosity to other people though personally he had never seemed to have any difficulty about being on Elvis's payroll.

'If there isn't any money then Elvis won't be dying,' I told them. 'Once he's disappeared you won't be able to send him money because you won't know where he is. So you have to find just over two million dollars and you have to find it now. We need one hundred thousand dollars in cash and two million in diamonds.' I asked for diamonds because I knew they would be easier to carry and easier to hide and pretty well impossible to trace. Two million dollars in notes would fill a suitcase and be difficult, if not impossible, to carry through customs. And I didn't want the Colonel sending money to a bank account because I didn't want a traceable paper trail connecting Elvis and the Colonel. Diamonds seemed a good, safe way to carry the money. I was confident that once we got to Paris I could slowly sell the diamonds to jewellers and then put the cash into a safe deposit box or, more usefully, a Swiss bank account in Elvis's new name.

'Impossible,' said the Colonel immediately. 'There isn't any money.'

'Then Elvis won't be dying,' I told them. I looked straight at the Colonel. 'And he's not going to be fit enough to do those shows in Las Vegas.'

'How much of this is for you? What's your cut?'

'You pay our expenses. But apart from expenses the whole two million is for Elvis. You'll make a fortune after his death. It's only fair that he has some money to live on. You're buying his past and his future.'

Two million dollars now would, I thought, give Elvis enough to live on. A quarter of it would buy him a decent apartment in Paris and the rest would give him enough income to live on for the rest of his life. I intended to stay with him for as long as he wanted, but I'd earn my own living. I was certainly not going to join the army of hangers-on who had, for years, lived on Elvis's generosity.

'I'll give the money to a Swiss banker in trust. All Elvis has to do is contact the man when he wants money.'

I frowned. I didn't like that idea at all.

'During the Second World War Goering gave all the money and art work he'd stolen to a Spanish nobleman,' said the Colonel. 'No paper trail at all. There was nothing to link the two men. Goering just told the Spaniard to keep it safe for him in case Germany lost the war and he was put in prison.'

'Goering trusted this guy?'

'Of course. If Germany had won the war would you have wanted to tell Goering he couldn't have his money back? And if Germany lost he'd collect the money when he could. Who would have the balls to say: 'No! You can't have your money, Herr Goering.'?'

'But Elvis isn't Goering,' I pointed out, rather unnecessarily. The Colonel clearly had some trick up his sleeve and I wasn't going to succumb that easily.

The Colonel sighed. 'I'll pay you two million if you can find a way to ensure that my boy dies and is properly certified,' he said at last. 'You'll have to think of some way to convince me, doctors and the world that the body in the coffin is Elvis and that he is truly dead.'

'Get the diamonds and the cash ready,' I said. 'We may have to move quickly.'

As I walked away I could hear the beginning of the inevitable argument. It was, of course, about money. When the Colonel and Vernon argued it was always about money.

Chapter Ten

Two days later I flew to England. I took with me a dozen passport sized photographs of Elvis and $20,000 in cash which the Colonel had rather reluctantly produced. The Colonel was always reluctant to part with money.

I had intended to take the photographic film with me and to have it developed in England there but in the end I decided it would be easier and simpler to develop the pictures myself. I took all the pictures with a cheap camera I found lying around. Elvis had some expensive equipment which was far too complicated for my purposes. We had some good fun taking the pictures; experimenting with different contact lenses and wigs. Elvis took the pictures of me. I experimented with a couple of expensive fake moustaches but abandoned them. They made me look like a man wearing cheap fake moustaches. Besides, Elvis had to have a moustache to try to hide his lip but I didn't need one. And two men wearing moustaches might attract a second look. I bought the printing and developing equipment from a photographic store in Memphis and was surprised how easy it was to create suitable pictures. Doing it this way I could pick out the photographs I wanted and completely cut out the risk of there being a picture on the roll that might look like Elvis. When I'd finished I burnt the negatives and the pictures I didn't want and put all the equipment I had bought, and no longer needed, into a garbage dump some way from Graceland. I didn't want to leave anything behind that could possibly turn out to be a clue.

I cannot remember why but I had planned to hire a car at Heathrow and to drive north on the M1 motorway, stopping at somewhere like Coventry or Northampton to find a cemetery and a couple of suitable gravestones. I needed two genuinely English names because Welsh or Scottish names would attract attention – and require us to speak in accents – but I didn't really mind whereabouts in England we originally came from. It was only when I was in the queue at the car rental desk that I suddenly realised that I really didn't need to leave London at all. There are, after all, plenty of cemeteries in the capital and I could travel to any of them by bus or tube without having to give anyone my name and credit card details.

It took me two days to find the information I wanted. I needed three gravestones which contained the names of two boys who had died young. The difficulty was that the gravestones I used had to contain the dates of birth I needed in order to obtain the two birth certificates. A surprising number of gravestones for young children contain the requisite flowery words, and perhaps a stone cherub or two but they don't include birth dates. And I had to ignore the graves of boys called Cyril, Cecil or anything similar. I didn't want to go through the rest of my life called Cyril and I knew Elvis would never agree to accept a passport in the name of Cecil.

I then found a small general store in Paddington where the owner would, for £5 a week, allow me to use his address as my own. I paid for three months in advance, using three crisp £20 notes which disappeared out of my hand fast enough to impress any magician, and in return he gave me a scruffy piece of paper torn out of an old invoice book confirming that I was entitled to pick up any mail addressed to the name I'd paid for. If I'd been willing to use my own name and show him some identification he would have charged me just £2 a week. I got the distinct impression that not many of his customers chose the cheaper option. I did pretty much the same thing at a small newsagent near Victoria station. For some reason or other the small shops which provide this informal service always seem to be located near to mainline railway stations. I suppose people coming to London but not having any fixed address look for something near to the station when they first arrive.

From then on everything was frighteningly simple and straightforward. I obtained the birth certificates I needed through the post and then filled in application forms for the two passports I needed. Naturally, I changed Elvis's hair and eye colour when I filled in that part of the form. I took the names of two doctors from the brass plates outside their surgeries and signed their names on the back of the photographs to confirm that the pictures were good likenesses of the individuals concerned. I chose doctors because they sign thousands of pieces of paper and cannot possibly ever remember what they have put their names to. A pleasant fellow at a Post Office where I picked up one of the application forms told me that I would have to wait two to three weeks for my new passport to arrive. It seemed a fair bet to assume that both passports would take roughly the same length of time.

Chapter Eleven

I would have quite liked to have stayed in England while I waited for the passports to turn up. A week or two in the Lake District, slumped in a small hotel on the edge of Lake Windermere, or few calming days in an old fashioned hostelry in Sidmouth in South Devon, would have done me more good than a bottle of Dr Collis Browne's inestimably efficacious tonic medicine, but I didn't have time for lolling about.

I flew back to the USA but instead of flying to Memphis I bought a return ticket to America and took a plane to New York. My plan was a simple one. Once we had arranged Elvis's official death I intended to take him somewhere quiet and secluded where he could lose weight and learn to live without the pills he was taking. My original plan had been to rent a farmhouse in some isolated part of the country but I quickly decided that would be exactly the wrong thing to do. People who live in the country always take a close interest in what is happening in their locality. If an isolated property were suddenly rented by two guys there were bound to be questions and there would be certain to be gossip. I decided that we would, instead, hide out in New York. The Queen of England could walk through Central Park wearing her crown and coronation regalia, and clutching the orb in one hand and the sceptre in the other, and attract the attention only of muggers.

I looked in the local papers for someone wanting to rent or sublet their apartment and eventually succeeded in finding a two bedroom apartment in a busy area of the city. The apartment was on the top floor and had a decent sized balcony which wasn't overlooked. I thought this was important because it meant that Elvis could get some of the air which the New Yorkers describe as their alternative to 'fresh'. There was also an available slot in the building's underground car park so we could drive straight in without having to find a parking space. The owner of the apartment, a young fellow working in the financial services industry, was being sent to South America by his firm. He didn't want to sell his flat but his loan arrangement didn't allow him to rent the place to a tenant. It was in his interest for the whole deal to be kept unofficial. I paid him cash for a whole year's rent, and the cost of the utilities, and he was delighted when I promised not to tell anyone about the deal. I told him he could have the telephone disconnected. I rented the flat furnished and he put his private things (those clothes, books, papers etc which he didn't need with him in South America) into a storage unit a couple of blocks away. I knew that our stay in New York would probably be the riskiest part of the whole operation but I was satisfied that the deal I'd made would be as safe as it could be.

The minute the apartment owner had gone I called in a locksmith and had new locks fitted – just in case the guy or an old girlfriend decided to try to let themselves in. When we left I put the new keys in the mailbox because there was no need to change the key to that. We certainly weren't expecting to receive any mail.

I hoped that after three months spent in hiding it would be safe for us to emerge and, using our new passports, to leave the country. It had always been clear that we really shouldn't stay in the USA longer than necessary. The obvious thing to do would have been to fly from an American airport direct to our ultimate destination. But I thought there were several problems with that idea. First, it would mean taking Elvis through the crowds and security barriers at an American airport. Passengers at airports always have far too much time on their hands and many seem to spend their spare hours trying to spot celebrities. I worried that Elvis, even slimmed down and disguised, would still be too recognisable. If just one fan saw him and started a stampede we would be finished. I had decided, therefore, to get him across the border into Canada and to fly from there to England. We would be flying with our new British passports and I thought we'd be fairly safe in leaving from a Canadian airport such as the ones in Montreal or Quebec. I'd have preferred to leave from a smaller airport some distance from the border with the USA but this would have meant even more travelling and some of Canada's smaller airports didn't fly direct to Britain back in the 1970's.

That still left us with the problem of leaving the United States and it seemed to me that Elvis and I would be wise to leave the country at a spot where we could lose ourselves amidst a mass of tourists. I quickly decided that Niagara was the perfect place to do that. I had to make all the plans because Elvis was too exhausted and drugged to decide anything more complicated than what he wanted to eat for breakfast. He was burnt out, utterly exhausted after years of struggling to remain the world's number one entertainer. Very few, if any, of his fans really understood just how ill Elvis had become.

I suspected then, and know now, that the early years, when he had been striving to make his mark on the music world, had been enjoyable and exhilarating. Like so many performers he had found that the really hard work comes when the climb is over and the task becomes not to ascend but to avoid falling. Elvis had risen so far, and so quickly, that the fight to remain focussed and sane was always going to be a hard one and his primary problem was that the people around him (particularly the closest two, the Colonel and the man he still called his `daddy') fed him only expectations and doubts and never offered him the support he truly needed. The Colonel was a great negotiator and he had, pretty well singlehandedly, created Elvis's reputation. But the Colonel was a rough, tough carnival barker who had little or no sympathy for weaknesses of any sort. And the infamous Memphis Mafia was largely composed of individuals who saw Elvis as a meal ticket; a seemingly unending source of money, cars and power. Back in those days anyone who made a telephone call from Graceland could expect to be treated like royalty. The sad thing was, however, that no one around him realised that although Elvis might have become the King he was, deep inside, still a nervous and exceptionally sensitive boy who lacked confidence and self-assurance. Most of the people living and working at Graceland were so worried about retaining their own position, their own status in the royal household, that they did not spend any time at all worrying about Elvis's physical and mental health.

I was well aware that immediately after Elvis's death there would be a good many people who wouldn't believe that their idol really had gone for ever. There would be massive news coverage of his 'death' and for a variety of reasons people would start spotting Elvis in all sorts of locations. Many fans wouldn't want to accept that Elvis was dead. Anyone who spotted a stranger who looked even vaguely like Elvis would be convinced that Elvis wasn't dead at all. And their immediate response would, of course, be to telephone their local newspaper, their favourite television station or their local radio station.

    I eventually decided that we would drive to New York in my car – for which I had originally paid cash in Chicago. I planned to sell the car in Montreal when we arrived in Canada and for us to then take the train to the airport in Quebec. I didn't think anyone would be able to trace the car because I intended to sell it for cash but if anyone did manage to trace our journey I thought it would be better for them to waste their time looking through passenger lists from Montreal rather than from Quebec.

Chapter Twelve

Using the other half of the return ticket I'd bought I then flew back to England. I checked with my two accommodation addresses when I got to London but neither of the passports had arrived. I wasn't really expecting them so I wasn't worried. I took the boat train from Victoria, crossed the channel on a ferry and took the train to Paris. I was still using my old, original British passport for all these journeys. I stayed in a small tourist hotel not far from the Place Vendome and paid cash for my room and breakfast. I then picked up a copy of a free magazine that carried advertisements for flats and services and looked at half a dozen furnished flats before renting one for Elvis and me to occupy if and when we finally reached Paris. I took the flat, a furnished top floor loft apartment in La Rue du Dr Finlay, a fairly quiet street in the unfashionable 15th arrondissement, for six months and paid in advance and in cash. People liked being paid cash in those days. At first I couldn't understand why the Parisians had named a street after a fictional Scottish doctor. But the landlord, a jolly little Belgian, explained to me that the street had been named after Dr Carlos J. Finlay, a Cuban doctor who is apparently commemorated for having discovered that yellow fever is transmitted by mosquitoes. The Parisians are fond of naming streets, avenues, boulevards and other thoroughfares after prominent individuals.

Anyone who has spent any time in Paris will, for example, have seen the name Felix Faure many times. He has more streets named after him than anyone else in French history but then not even Napoleon, that most famous and esteemed Frenchman of them all, died in such a flamboyant version of flagrante delicto. After a successful career as an industrialist Faure became President of France's Third Republic and is famous for the fact that he died, literally, in office. In the sort of history books which are used in schools his death is described as `sudden' and `unexpected' and it is usually reported that he died at his desk wearing a frock coat and a high, starched collar. What the history books don't report is that

Faure wasn't poring over State papers when he died but had a naked girl kneeling between his legs with his hands caressing her head. When he reached the vital moment the unfortunate politician had a heart attack and died so quickly that his fingers were left clutching the poor girl's hair. She could only be released when some of her hair was cut away. When the news first hit the streets of Paris Faure immediately became a national hero. In most other countries the electors frown on such behaviour but in France they regard it as quite laudable and the authorities immediately set about commemorating his magnificent life (and death) by naming just about every available road and building in his memory. Today, Faure even has his own Metro station.

The area I'd chosen for our temporary, first lodgings was largely occupied by locals who wanted somewhere close to the city centre but who could not afford the extraordinary prices for apartments in the 7th arrondissement on the other side of the Champ de Mars. There weren't many Americans or Britons living there at the time and that suited me perfectly. The landlord, who apparently owned the whole building and several other properties in the area, did not seem to me to be the sort of man likely to care overmuch if his tenants did not appear for several months as long as they had paid their rent. My plan was that Elvis and I would stay there for a few weeks and then find something more permanent which we both liked. After I'd collected the keys from the landlord I stocked the apartment with some basic groceries so that when we arrived we could at least use the loo and make a cup of coffee. I also bought an armful of towels and bed linen from a small shop I found nearby.

I celebrated alone with a double espresso in a café close to the nearby Eiffel Tower. It occurred to me for the first time that there was real irony in Elvis moving to France under an assumed identity; driven out of his own country by critics and over-demanding fans who expected him to stay svelte for ever. The French are probably the only people who do not turn on their heroes in the way that the British and the Americans are prone to do. The result is that their great heroes enjoy much longer careers and remain heroes until they die. Why are we so cruel to our heroes? Why do journalists and fans treat their heroes so harshly and so unforgivingly? Why do they put their heroes up on such high pedestals and then deliberately rock the pedestals until the inevitable happens? We have no word in the English language to match the German 'shadenfreud' but I can't help feeling that we should have. The British and the Americans seem to be the only people on the planet who get great pleasure from seeing their heroes cut down to human size. Maybe we cannot stand to see our heroes getting older because the very signs of their ageing remind us that we too must be losing our youth.

After two nights in Paris I took the train and boat back to London where I found that, to my intense relief, both new passports were waiting for my collection. I then hid the new passports in a money belt in case my luggage was searched and flew back to the United States. No one searched my luggage or me and so the passports remained safe and undisturbed. If they had been found the whole plan would have been destroyed and I would have had some very difficult questions to answer. But they weren't, it wasn't and I didn't.

Chapter Thirteen

While I had been away I had not dared to ring Elvis to tell him how things were going because I had feared that the conversation might have proved incriminating. Elvis had long been convinced that his telephones were tapped and I shared his feelings about this. But despite his suspicions about phone tapping Elvis still remained frighteningly innocent and naïve, and quite likely to put us both up to our necks in hot soup. I could imagine the conversation we would have had.

'Hello Elvis.'
'Oh Hi! How's Europe?'
'It's very well, thank you. Full of foreigners but it's bearing up.'
'Did you manage to get the fake passports?'
'The what?'
'The phoney passports. Did you manage to get them OK? Did you find two dead babies whose names we could use?'

So I hadn't telephoned and had stayed completely out of touch. As a result I had a nasty shock when I got back to Memphis and I found that Elvis had changed his mind about dying. The Colonel, God bless his Dutch ancestors, had apparently decided that the risks were too high and that I would not be able to think of a way to fake Elvis's death convincingly. He had apparently also managed to improve the Las Vegas contract he had already signed. And so he had decided that he could, after all, make as much out of a live Elvis as out of a dead one.

After chasing around London, Paris and New York for several weeks I was, to say the very least, not terribly amused by this change of heart. In fact, I was pretty damned cross and if I had managed to find the old goat there and then it would have been the Colonel, rather than a fake Elvis, who would have been taking a trip in a hearse.

I also found a string of messages from Donald Case, the Elvis impersonator I'd met. They sounded urgent.

Chapter Fourteen

'I had a heart attack,' said Donald. He didn't look well. In fact, if he hadn't been talking to me I would have believed anyone who had told me he'd died. His skin was sallow and he was constantly sweating. He was sitting in an easy chair. But, ill as he looked, he was still a dead ringer for Elvis.

'Shouldn't you be in hospital?' I asked him. He was living in a small motel on the outskirts of Memphis. It was a dingy and miserable place in which to be ill. And it occurred to me that it would be a dingy and miserable place in which to die.

'I don't want to be in hospital,' he told me. 'I don't want to die with tubes sticking out of me.' He spoke in bursts of no more than two or three words a time. In between he took desperate, gasping breaths.

'Are you in pain?'

He shook his head. 'They gave me a good supply of pills.' He waved a hand towards an array of bottles sitting on the table beside him.

I looked at the pills. Demerol. Valium. Codeine. I knew the names because they were the drugs Elvis was taking. There were other pills too, most of which I recognised.

'They're good painkillers,' he said. 'The Demerol are quite strong.'

'Pethidine,' I said. 'A sort of morphine.' I'd done a bit of research because of Elvis.

Donald nodded.

'Did the doctors say how long you'll have to take things easy? How long before you're back on stage?'

He shook his head. 'I've got a week. Maybe two.'

'Before you're back on stage?'

'Before I'm dead.'

I looked around the room. It was squalid. The wallpaper was peeling off the walls and the carpet had long since lost its thread and its colour. It was no place to live or to die.

'How's Elvis?' asked Donald.

'Exhausted,' I told him. 'The Colonel wants him to do more shows. But he's in no state to do anything in public.'

'As fat as me?'

I nodded.

'And as out of shape?'

I nodded again.

'He should retire now so that the fans can remember him the way he was.'

'The Colonel won't let him.'

I would never have shared these secrets with anyone else. But Donald was different. And he was dying.

Donald, who knew all about the Colonel, of course, just closed his eyes in understanding.

I told Donald about my plan to fake Elvis's death. I explained why I thought it was the only way Elvis could survive. Donald didn't need to be told my plan. He didn't even force me to put it into words for him.

'You could use my body,' said Donald. 'I'd be honoured. Come and get me when I'm gone and lie me down in Elvis's bed.' He smiled at the thought. 'For an Elvis impersonator it would be a dream come true. The ultimate victory in the ultimate competition.' He smiled. 'I would actually be Elvis.'

It was as simple as that.

'Elvis and the Colonel have gone off the idea,' I told Donald. 'But maybe they'll change their minds when they realise that there is a way we can fool the world.'

'Oh I do hope so,' said Donald.

'Whatever they decide you're not going to stay here,' I told him. 'You're coming to Graceland.'

Donald looked at me as if I'd promised him his own cloud, gold harp and a seat next to God. 'Can you do that?'

'You can use my room,' I told him. 'I can easily tell the maids not to go in there. I'll tell them I've got a girlfriend staying with me and that she's very shy and sleeps a lot. Something like that. They won't mind having less work to do.'

Donald smiled and reached out and touched my hand. 'You've made my life worthwhile.'

Chapter Fifteen

'The Colonel says I have to do this tour,' said Elvis, glumly. 'It's all planned. The guys are packing the suitcases.' It was just before midday and it was unusual to see him up and about at that time. He was wearing a pale orange jump suit and eating bacon sandwiches, one of his favourite meals. The bacon was very crisp, almost burnt, and the butter on the bread seemed to have been put there with a spoon rather than a knife. There must have been a thousand calories in each sandwich and Elvis had already worked his way through three of them. This was the fourth.

'You don't have to do anything you don't want to do,' I told him. 'You're Elvis Presley for heaven's sake. If America had royalty you would be it; the entire royal family. You're more loved than any single person in the history of America.'

'We need the money,' said Elvis. He put the rest of the sandwich into his mouth and chewed. He was clearly eating for comfort but the food didn't seem to be comforting him. His eyes were glazed and he had obviously taken his usual cocktail of tranquillisers, anti-depressants, painkillers and sleeping tablets. He seemed to have got much, much worse in the few weeks I'd been away. I couldn't help thinking that if he kept on the way he was we wouldn't have to fake his death. I wondered if the Colonel had factored in the chances of his 'boy' dying on stage in the middle of 'Don't be Cruel' or 'Heartbreak Hotel'. 'The Colonel says we can't meet the payroll unless I do the shows.'

'Elvis, you can't really need the money,' I told him. 'You can live on your royalties. Cut your expenses and you'll be rich.'

He shook his head and reached for another thousand calorie bacon sandwich. 'I can't do that,' he said. 'All these people rely on me. They've got families too.' It would, I thought, be a race between his heart and his colon. A heart attack or cancer? I watched in horror as he took a huge bite out of the sandwich.

'You're not responsible for all these people for ever,' I told him. 'Sack us all and relax for a while.' He chewed, apparently without pleasure. 'I can't do that,' he said, when he'd finished chewing. He shook his head. 'I wouldn't have no people round me if I did that.' He took another huge bite.

And suddenly I realised that Elvis was, more than anything, terrified of being alone. For years he had been literally buying friends and playmates. And without them who would there be?

'I missed you,' he said suddenly, and unexpectedly. He had a third of an uneaten sandwich in his hand but instead of taking a bite he put it down on the huge serving plate. This was, for him, a rare move. If he picked up something he was going to eat then he usually ate it all. There were four other sandwiches on the plate which sat on a portable plate warmer.

I grinned at him. 'I missed you too, you fat, greedy bastard.'

He looked at me sheepishly but didn't say anything for a while. 'No one else ever talks to me like you do,' he said. 'Everyone else talks to me as though they're frightened of me. It ain't natural.'

'Most of them are frightened of losing their jobs,' I pointed out. 'You do have a temper. You've been known to fire people who've annoyed you.'

'Yeah.' He looked at the remains of the sandwich but didn't pick it up.

'You can't let them keep bullying you into doing things you really don't want to do,' I told him. 'It'll never end unless you do something to end it soon.' I pointed to the pile of bacon sandwiches that still remained. 'You keep eating and you keep popping pills because you can't cope with your life.'

'You want me to do that dying thing?'

'No,' I said loudly. 'I don't want you to do anything you don't want to do. The best thing you could do would be to fire everyone and tell the Colonel that you're retiring. Or that you're taking a year off. Maybe you'll feel better in a year's time.'

'I'd like to do that.' He picked up the sandwich he'd been eating, looked at it, nibbled at a small piece of burnt bacon, and then put it back down on the plate. 'I'd like to do that,' he said.

'But?'

He looked at me, puzzled.

'But what? Why don't you retire? You don't have to retire permanently.'

'It wouldn't work. I couldn't do it.'

'Why not?'

'The Colonel wouldn't let me. And I'd feel too bad about all the folk I'd have to fire.'

'You're going to kill yourself if you keep going the way you are.'

He looked at me and then closed his eyes for a while.

'I'd feel too bad,' he said. 'Most of these folk would never get proper jobs again.'

'Most of these folk have never had proper jobs!' I pointed out.

Almost imperceptibly, Elvis nodded. He knew I was right.

'If you carry on like this you're going to kill yourself for them.'

'I dreamt a lot about that dying thing,' said Elvis. 'I really want to do it.' He touched the sandwich and broke off a small piece of buttered bread. He put the bread into his mouth and chewed on it. 'Were you lying to me when you told me I could lose all that weight in three months?'

'No.'

'What about the pills? I hate taking all these damned pills. I really do. But I take them because they help me forget the shows and that book those guys wrote.'

'I think you'll be able to kick the pills if you leave Graceland. While I've been away I've been reading about the drugs you take. They're addictive but you can get off them.'

'Will you help me?'

'Yes. I'll help you.'

He looked at me. 'Why? Why do all this for me?'

'Because I like you,' I told him. 'I remember the Elvis I knew in Paris. You'll never be that young and slim again. But you can get back to being something like the man you were. And I'll help you because you're a kind man. You took me in when I had nowhere else to go.' Then I'll smiled. 'And I'll help you because what else am I doing with my life? This will be a huge adventure.'

'The Colonel says you want me to run away because you need to hide to get away from that guy whose wife you screwed.'

'The Colonel is lying,' I told him bluntly. 'I can keep away from him just by going to Europe. Besides, the guy in Chicago has probably forgotten about me by now. His wife will have been through at least half a dozen new lovers.'

'She sounds like a whore.'

'She should have been. She wasn't a very good interior designer.'

'He says you asked for a million dollars for yourself.'

'Then that's another lie.' I felt myself going red with fury. The Colonel would do anything to get his own way. 'Ask Vernon,' I told him. 'He was there when I saw the Colonel.'

'I don't need to do that.'

'Yes you do,' I said. I got up and walked away. I found Vernon Presley watching television and told him Elvis needed to hear something from him. Together, we went back to where Elvis was sitting.

'When the Colonel and I were talking about Elvis dying did I ask for money for myself?'

'No,' said Vernon without hesitation. 'He asked you what you wanted and you said you didn't want anything.'

'I didn't believe him,' said Elvis quietly, when his father had gone back to his television programme.

'The Colonel has done great things for you,' I told Elvis. 'But now he will do anything he can to keep you working. He needs the money.'

'I've heard he owes a lot of money. Millions. And those people in Vegas don't like holding IOUs. You can't spend IOUs.'

We sat without speaking. It seemed as though we had been like that for a long while. But it probably wasn't more than a couple of minutes.

'The Colonel also said there's no way that you can fool people into thinking I'm dead.'

'The Colonel is wrong about that too,' I told him. 'Come to my room and I'll show you why.'

Elvis frowned and looked bewildered.

'I'll show you the man who will be your dead body,' I told him.

Chapter Sixteen

Elvis was always good with fans. He respected them and recognised that it was their support which had made him a star. His very special talent, and the Colonel's curious, unique marketing genius were the foundation stones upon which his career had been built but Elvis knew that it is, of course, the fans who ultimately decide who will thrive and who will die in the piranha world of show business. Elvis knew that there have been many talented and skilled individuals whose stars have flamed but briefly or never flamed at all. It was, I believed then and know now, that it was this rare understanding which was destroying him. Other stars, filled to the brim with self-confidence and hubristic in all that they do, do not have the imagination to see themselves falling from the sky. Elvis, however, knew that his status as the King was threatened every day by would-be usurpers and by the fickleness of the fans who had put him on the throne.

When Elvis walked into my room and saw himself lying on top of my bed he was unable to speak. I introduced the two men to each other. One was overawed, thinking perhaps that he had already died and gone to heaven, and the other, accustomed to seeing caricatures of himself on stage and television, was stunned to see a man whom he had last seen when he had stood in his bathroom and shaved one of the best known faces in the world. Donald was wearing his worn and stained stage outfit. He'd insisted on wearing it when I'd driven him to Graceland. His pill bottles were standing on my bedside table and his battered cardboard suitcase, containing all his worldly goods including the contents of his storage locker, was still standing, unopened, on a chair. He had checked out of the motel and I'd paid his bill.

It did not occur to me until many months later but that meeting made it much, much easier for Elvis to lose his excess weight during the three months after his death. Seeing a three dimensional version of himself, and realising just how obese he had become, made Elvis face a fact that he, and most of those close to him, had done everything possible to ignore or disguise.

Donald tried to get up off the bed. I expect he felt that it was wrong for him to be lying down when the King was standing. Elvis bent down, reached out, put a hand on Donald's shoulder to prevent him moving, and murmured a few words. I can't remember exactly what he said. Donald smiled and looked at Elvis. 'Not a bad likeness, eh? But I think I let my sideburns grow a little too bushy.' I remember him saying that because I remember looking and thinking that he was right. You could only really tell when the two men were right next to each other.

And then Donald died.

He gave a huge sigh, grabbed at Elvis's arm with his right hand and at the bed coverlet with his left hand, and died. I don't suppose many men have actually died touching their dream.

'He needs a doctor,' said Elvis, untangling himself. 'He's having some sort of seizure.'

I took Donald's wrist and felt for a pulse. Nothing. I felt for a pulse in his neck. Nothing. The excitement of meeting Elvis had been too much for him.

'He's dead,' I told Elvis.

Elvis just looked at me and then back at Donald. He backed away from the bed.

'He came here knowing that he was dying,' I told him. 'And no one ever died happier.'

'Call Dr Nick!' said Elvis.

'It's too late for Dr Nick,' I told him. 'You have to decide now if you want to go.'

Elvis looked at me. He didn't understand.

'Donald is a dead ringer for you,' I pointed out unnecessarily. 'He came here to be your dead body.'

'I just died?'

'If you want to, you just died.'

When I'd brought Donald to Graceland I had not expected him to die quite so quickly. I had thought that the poor fellow might have a week or two to enjoy living at the house. And I had expected to have some time to plan Elvis's death. But this was a once in a lifetime chance.

'What am I doing dying here? On your bed? How do we explain this?'

'Do you want to die or do you want to do the tour? You have to decide now.'

Elvis didn't hesitate. He immediately grasped that this was his one chance to escape from a life that was killing him. He told me later that the fact that there was a dead man lying on my bed had helped him make the decision. He knew damned well that unless he changed his lifestyle, and changed it quickly and dramatically, he too would soon be dead. And looking at Donald had made him realise just how absurd he himself would now look in one of his stage suits.

'Where do we go if I die?' he asked me.

'We go to an apartment in New York for three months. Then we cross the border into Canada and fly to Europe. I've got an apartment in Paris waiting for us. I have new passports ready for us.'

Elvis looked at me. It was, of course, a huge decision. A far bigger decision than most people are ever required to make. And it required a good deal of trust.

'Elvis just died,' he said.

I picked up the phone and rang the Colonel, who was in Portland helping to organise the coming tour. He and some of Elvis's people were booking rooms and fixing up security. The absence of the Colonel could have been disastrous but at least Vernon was at Graceland. He was in my room in less than five minutes. I put the Colonel on the speaker phone so that we could all talk to him and hear what he said. Donald looked so much like Elvis that for a moment Vernon wasn't entirely sure who had died. It did occur to me that if even Elvis's own father couldn't tell them apart we weren't going to have any problems with anyone else.

'Are you sure you want to walk away from being Elvis?' the Colonel asked Elvis. 'You can never come back.'

'I want to go,' said Elvis firmly.

'Is there anyone in your bedroom?' the Colonel asked him.

'Ginger,' said Elvis. Ginger was his fiancée.

'Damn.'

'We can tell Ginger,' said Elvis. 'She won't tell anyone.'

'We can't risk telling anyone else,' I told Elvis. I hated telling him this. I knew how much he cared for Ginger. It seemed, and was, cruel not to tell her the truth but I didn't want to risk telling anyone who didn't have to know. We didn't tell Elvis's cousin Billy, either. Even an unintentional, careless slip would have been disastrous.

'We'll have to get him out of this damned silly suit,' said Vernon. He was struggling to remove the stage outfit from Donald.

'Cut if off,' I told him. I took out a pocket knife and handed it to Vernon.

'Colonel, I hate to bring this up at a time like this,' I said. 'But Elvis is going to need money. And we need it now.'

'How much?'

'The same as before. A hundred thousand in cash, to cover our initial expenses, and two million dollars in diamonds for Elvis.'

'Impossible.'

'It's not impossible. And it's what we agreed.'

'Vernon,' said the Colonel. 'Does this body look like our boy?'

'You wouldn't know the difference,' said Vernon.

'OK,' sighed the Colonel. 'Give him the money, Vernon.'

'All of it?'

'Of course all of it. One hundred thousand dollars in cash and the diamonds.'

'The diamonds are worth two million?' I asked.

'That was wholesale. They're worth more than that. Probably double. Do you think I'd cheat my boy?'

I didn't answer the question. I wasn't the only one who thought that the Colonel had been cheating Elvis all his life.

'We'll need to burn those clothes,' I said to Vernon. He turned to me. 'Has he got any more clothes?'

'He?'

'The dead guy.'

'Donald.'

'Whoever. Has he got any more clothes?'

'They're all in that suitcase.'

'We have to burn everything. And his pills.'

'Is anyone going to miss him?' asked the Colonel, from Portland.

'No.'

'Does he have a house? Apartment? Wife? Family? Car?'

'No to all of those.'

Elvis picked up the bottles of pills and examined them carefully. 'I take these,' he said, looking at one bottle. He picked up a second bottle. 'And these. Darn it the man was even taking the same pills as me.' He started to collect up the bottles.

'That's what made him so perfect,' I said. I took the pills off him and put them back on the bedside cabinet.

'Pity to waste them,' said Elvis, looking rather longingly at the drugs. 'I could use them.'

'No!' I said.

'I could put the tablets into some of my containers,' he replied immediately, 'we must have tons of empty ones.'

'No. You don't need them.'

'This is a very stressful time for me.'

I turned to face him and looked him straight in the eye. 'This is the easy bit. If you think this is stressful then you should stay alive and do the shows.'

Elvis swallowed hard. He wasn't accustomed to people arguing with him, let alone anyone other than the Colonel telling him what he could or should do or not do with his life. He looked disappointed, like a kid who has been told that Christmas has been postponed and may even be cancelled altogether.

'I can't do any more shows,' he said quietly. And I believed him. I think that at that moment he would have slit his own wrists rather than go out on stage and sing 'Hound Dog' or 'All Shook Up' one more time. He was clearly completely burnt out and at that moment I felt as sorry for him as I had ever felt for anyone I'd ever met.

I put my hand on his upper arm. 'OK,' I said softly. 'Is there anything you need to take with you?'

'I need to take some clothes.'

'No you don't. You're never again going to wear jump suits, silk shirts or anything decorated with tassels or sequins.'

'I'm not?'

'You're not. Is there anything else you need?'

'Jewellery?'

'No.'

'Books? Tapes?'

'We'll buy whatever you need.'

'I could write out a list of what I want and the Colonel could send them on to me. One of the guys could bring them in an unmarked van.'

'No.'

'Why not?'

'Because then one of the guys would know that you're still alive. And they'd know where to find us.'

'Yeah. I guess so.' Elvis thought for a moment. He sighed. 'Maybe I should just leave all this stuff to you?'

'Might be a good idea,' I said. I looked at my watch. Donald had been dead for nearly ten minutes. I wondered how long it would take Elvis to learn how to make all his own decisions and take control of his life again. I didn't want to find myself running his life as the Colonel had done for so long.

'Help me stuff these clothes in this bag,' said Vernon.

I turned round. Vernon had removed all Donald's clothes and was stuffing them into a large laundry bag which he had found in my bathroom. He'd tipped the clothes that had been in it onto the floor.

'How are you leaving?' the Colonel asked me. I was surprised at how calm he was. Vernon, on the other hand, looked as if he were only a nudge away from a complete nervous breakdown.

'I'll drive out with Elvis under a pile of cardboard boxes in the back of my car,' I told him. The fans outside never looked twice at me or my car. I doubt if any of them had the faintest idea who I was or what I did at Graceland. I would have preferred to put Elvis into the boot but I didn't think he'd fancy that. But if he lay down in the rear foot well and I piled a lot of empty cardboard boxes on top of him it would look as if I were simply transporting boxes full of something boring. I'd brought Donald into Graceland in exactly the same way and no one had taken the slightest bit of interest.

'Why can't I go out under a rug?' asked Elvis. 'I've done the under a rug thing lots of times. It ain't too bad. I just lie down on the back seat and you throw a rug over me. I can stay like that for hours.'

'If fans see me leaving Graceland with a rug thrown over a body in the back seat they'll know it's you,' I told him. 'And then when it's announced that you've died the rumours will really start.'

'We're going to need a death certificate!' said Vernon suddenly. He was still struggling to cram Donald's stage suit into the laundry bag.

'The coroner will give us the certificate,' said the Colonel, firmly.

I glanced at Donald and suddenly realised that he was still wearing his underpants and his socks. The underpants were grey, frayed and none too clean and the socks were odd and had holes in the heels and the toes. They were certainly not clothes Elvis would have worn.

'We need him naked,' I told Vernon.

'I'm not touching those!' protested Vernon. He glared at me. 'You take them off.'

I removed Donald's underpants and socks and put them on top of the rest of the clothing in the laundry sack. I then added the bottles of pills.

'His wiener is smaller than mine, said Elvis suddenly.

'No one is going to look at that,' I assured him. He was right, though. Even allowing for the fact that he was naked and dead Donald's wiener did not look impressive. It was not the sort of wiener a rock star would be proud to own. I didn't say anything but I thought that Donald's testicles looked a trifle undersized too.

'Someone is going to measure it and take photographs and sell 'em to one of the supermarket tabloids,' said Elvis in a panic.

'They won't,' I assured him, though I confess that I wasn't entirely sure that he wasn't right.

'Since Ginger is in the bedroom we'll have to carry the body up to Elvis's bathroom,' said Vernon. 'We'll put a pair of Elvis's pyjamas on him and leave him there for someone to find.'

He and I tried to lift the body off the bed. We could just about move him but we couldn't carry him. I wasn't surprised. Donald was truly huge. He looked like a whale, who had been blown inshore and had somehow been beached on my bed.

'Are you sure the coroner is going to give us a certificate?' asked Vernon, holding his back with both hands and looking down at the body.

'If you see a dead, fat man who looks like Elvis, on the floor in Elvis's bathroom who are you going to think it is?' asked the Colonel's disembodied voice from the telephone receiver. 'President Nixon, the bloke from the gas station down the road or Elvis? Besides, you and I are going to confirm that this is Elvis's body. No one is going to argue with us.'

'Take your point,' said Vernon. 'But there's no call to be sassy. Just you remember that now that Elvis is dead you ain't managing nobody.'

'My verbal contract with Elvis covers him dead or alive!' insisted the Colonel.

I felt glad that I wasn't going to be around to watch this battle develop.

'I ain't dead yet,' said Elvis. 'Elvis ain't dead until I've left the building.'

We all looked at him.

'You're going to have to help us carry Donald' I told him. 'Stay where you are,' I told the Colonel. 'I'll be back in a couple of minutes.

'I'm not touching a dead body!' said Elvis.

'You have to,' I told him.

He reached out and touched Donald's leg. 'It feels kind of funny.'

'We can't carry him without you.'

'I need gloves. I can't carry him unless I'm wearing gloves.'

I found a pair of leather gloves. Elvis looked at them. 'These are old.'

'I've had them a long time. Put the damned gloves on, Elvis.'

Elvis put on the gloves. And then Elvis, his father and I carried Donald from my bedroom to Elvis's bathroom. I was terrified that we would meet someone on the way, or that when we got there Ginger, woken by all our huffing and puffing, would wander in to see what was happening.

But we were lucky.

No one saw us. And we successfully managed to deposit Donald on the bathroom floor. Elvis took a pair of his gold pyjamas out of a cupboard and Vernon and I managed to put them onto the corpse. Vernon said he'd go back after we'd gone and make sure that everything looked OK.

'In the unlikely event of anyone noticing that I'm not here just tell them that I left and you don't know where I've gone,' I told Vernon Presley. 'Empty my room and throw everything into the incinerator.' I suspected that, in the chaos and confusion that would inevitably follow the discovery of Elvis's body, no one at Graceland would notice that I'd gone and I was certain that no one would care.

'I've got to say goodbye to Lisa Marie,' said Elvis.

I looked at him. He was serious.

'You can't,' I said quietly. I felt awful.

'Why not? She's my daughter.'

'You can't,' I repeated. 'If you tell her 'goodbye' she will know that you're not dead. And she will tell someone.'

There was silence for a moment. I could hear voices somewhere in the house. They sounded as if they were a thousand miles away, maybe on another planet, perhaps in another galaxy. I could feel my heart beating at my rib cage as though it were trying to escape from my chest.

'Not if I tell her not to say anything,' said Elvis, desperately.

'You can't expect her to do that,' I said so quietly that I could hardly hear myself speak. 'You can't. You really can't.'

There were tears in Elvis's eyes. I thought I knew how he felt but I didn't, of course. No one could know what he was going through.

'If I stay I have to do the tour don't I?'

I nodded.

'Be humiliated.'

I looked at him. 'Maybe it doesn't matter. The money will be good. You can cut your expenses here and save some money for the future.'

'I can't do it,' he said. His voice was flat. 'I can't do the tour. She'll be ashamed of me. The fans will be embarrassed. I'll be ashamed and embarrassed.' He paused. 'And I could never sack people here. If I go there will be plenty of money for everyone, won't there?'

I nodded.

'Let's go. Let's get out of here.'

I took Elvis out to where my car was parked. It was a Ford of such undistinguished parentage that I don't think I ever knew what model it was. It was, I seem to remember, a sort of blueish green in colour though I am sure the manufacturers had some fancier name for it. The abdicating King of Rock and Roll lay down in the back foot well and I covered him with a dozen empty cardboard boxes in which food supplies had been delivered to the house. When I'd finished I couldn't see out of the back window. Three or four minutes later Vernon appeared holding a cheap supermarket plastic bag. He handed it to me and I looked inside. The bag contained a good many hundred dollar bills and a small leather pouch. There wasn't time to count the money or to look at the diamonds. I had to assume that Vernon would not rip off his son.

'Is this all of it?'

'That's all of it.'

'You might have put it into a briefcase.'

'You didn't say you wanted a case. Briefcases cost money.'

I looked at him. 'Thanks, Vernon.' I wouldn't miss the Colonel and I wouldn't miss Elvis's father. I was glad to be leaving. I'd had enough of the Graceland life.

Elvis's father stuck his head close to my window. 'Good luck, son,' he said, speaking to the body underneath the cardboard boxes in the back of the car.

'You too, daddy,' said a muffled Elvis.

I let out the clutch and put my foot on the accelerator. Four or five minutes later we drove out through the Graceland gates for the last time. The fans took absolutely no notice of me, the car or the pile of boring looking cardboard boxes stacked across the rear seats. They were too busy peering through the now open gates to see the man they really wanted to see. I didn't look back and Elvis couldn't. Our new life had started. It was going to be a long, hard journey. I'm not sure that either of us would have started on it if we had known just how long and hard it would be.

Chapter Seventeen

It is just over one thousand miles from Memphis, Tennessee to New York and I can remember every mile of that damned journey as though it were yesterday.

After we had driven for a couple of hours or so we crossed into Kentucky and I stopped at the side of the road. I can't remember the name of the town but there were half a dozen huge dumpsters parked nearby. Elvis and I took the cardboard boxes out of the car, flattened them and tossed them into the nearest dumpster. Fortunately, I had the wit to check the boxes because one of them still had a sticky address label attached to it. I peeled off the label, screwed it up and threw it down a nearby storm grating.

Before we continued on the journey I gave Elvis a flowered print dress, a long blonde wig and a pair of very feminine sunglasses. I told him he had to take off his trousers. Elvis made a good woman. He looked rather like Jane Russell, but without the generous, bra filling superstructure. He complained that he looked very flat chested. I told him his legs were hairy. Fortunately, he was wearing tasselled loafers and not cowboy boots. There wasn't time for a more sophisticated disguise. I knew that if we were stopped by the police we would have no chance but I wanted to get to New York as quickly as I safely could. The important thing was that no one saw anyone looking even remotely like Elvis go into the apartment in New York.

I had estimated that it would take us around 24 hours to drive from Memphis to New York and on more than one occasion during that seemingly interminable journey I wished I'd picked somewhere closer for our hideout. We would undoubtedly have been able to do it in less time if I hadn't been so anxious that we didn't break the speed limit. To his credit Elvis didn't complain once and seemed to accept that New York was a logical destination. I had explained to him that I thought we would be safer hiding out in an apartment in a big city rather than on a deserted farm in the middle of nowhere.

Elvis and I shared the driving and apart from occasional halts to take on fuel and the inevitable fast food supplies we didn't stop for the first 12 hours. When Elvis needed to take a leak we stopped on lonely stretches of road. Never exceeding the speed limit we drove through Kentucky, West Virginia and, finally, entered Pennsylvania. We had no real idea what was happening in Memphis or how the media were dealing with Elvis's death though every time I stopped to buy gas or food I couldn't help noticing that the television news was dominated by Elvis's death. The serving staff could hardly drag their eyes away from the screens to serve me. I reckon that at least half the people I saw were either actually crying or looked as though they were about to start crying. We both agreed that listening to the radio news would distract us and I knew it would obviously distress Elvis and so we entirely missed the first day of news. As the traffic got heavier I told Elvis to climb into the back and to lie slumped as though sleeping. Even though he must have been buzzing with adrenalin he went to sleep almost straight away. I filled up the tank and bought two boxes of doughnuts and a few bottles of soda at a rest stop when we had around two hundred miles to go.

Travelling from Memphis to New York we gained an hour because of the time difference. We left Graceland at lunchtime and we arrived in New York in the early afternoon the following day. As we drove through West Virginia I thought about finding somewhere to stop for a while so that we could arrive at the apartment building after midnight. But eventually I decided that this would increase the risks instead of reducing them.

I remember we entered the New York flat at 3.55 pm and we did so without anyone noticing us. I know the time because there was a huge clock in the hallway that always kept perfect time. I drove straight into the underground car park beneath the building and we took the lift up to the top floor where the apartment was situated. We needed a hot meal so I put four doughnuts into the oven while Elvis turned on the television set and sat down on the sofa to catch up with the news of his death.

The next twelve hours were, without a doubt, the worst of both our lives. We were utterly exhausted by the journey. We were filthy and needed showers. We had survived on fatty junk food and felt slightly nauseous. We needed to rest.

But we sat there for hour after hour and watched the awful story of Elvis's fake death unfold. He was furious with a report that Donald's body had been found in the bathroom with his trousers around his ankles. We never did understand just why and how that happened. Maybe Vernon thought it would add verisimilitude to a scene that needed nothing. But for most of the time Elvis cried. He sobbed when he saw his father and he cried when he saw the Colonel, whom he thought of as another father, and he cried most of all when the television stations showed shots of his daughter Lisa Marie. A hundred times he wanted to call her on the telephone. And a hundred times I had to stop him. He repeatedly wanted to know why we hadn't told her the truth before he'd left. I repeatedly had to explain why it would have been cruel to share such a secret with a nine year old girl. I had to remind him, too, that the Colonel had told me that Elvis's professional life would become ever harder and that Lisa Marie would have to put up with teasing and abuse from kids at school as her overweight, out of condition father struggled to keep his career going. He cried when he saw fans crying outside Graceland. He cried when celebrities spoke in kindly terms about his career. He cried when fans explained that they would always remember exactly where they were, what they were wearing and what they were doing when Elvis died. He cried when the television companies showed shots of him performing or showed clips of his movies. He cried when industry insiders forecast that his records would fill the following week's Top Twenty charts. He cried when analysts talked about the financial chaos he had left behind and how his death would fill the Presley coffers. He cried and cried and cried and cried at everything and nothing. He flicked from channel to channel and at least once every ten minutes or so I had to physically prevent him from picking up the telephone and ringing a television studio to tell them that he was still alive. Quite a few people who were interviewed insisted that they didn't think the person in the coffin was Elvis.

    At one point Elvis took out a derringer which he'd stashed in one of his socks. He aimed the damned thing at the television set and would have fired it if I hadn't taken it away from him. It certainly wouldn't have been the first time he'd shot a television set. I had to explain to him that although it might have been acceptable for Elvis Presley to shoot television sets it wasn't acceptable for ordinary citizens. At Graceland he was always shooting inanimate objects. He once shot his wardrobe and put neat bullet holes in 16 neatly ironed shirts. He really did have a great affection for firearms. I remember one of the Memphis Mafia once telling me that Elvis had demanded a tour of the FBI building. At the start of the tour he and six friends were told that they had to hand over their guns. Naturally, Elvis didn't take any notice. He toured one of the most security conscious buildings in the world with two guns in his pockets. A day after the incident with the derringer I found out that he'd also managed to bring a 0.25 automatic with him.

'It feels like I'm dying over and over again,' said Elvis after watching the television news for several hours without a break. It occurred to me that dying for real is easy. Even the most stupid people can manage it; sometimes at the first attempt. But dying and staying alive is difficult in so many different ways; it requires imagination as well as the will to deceive but most of all it requires a strength of mind and purpose and an ability to cope with enormous emotional upheavals. For Elvis these demands were enormous because his dying was being done in public.

I didn't know what to say. For the first time I really began to have doubts about whether or not we'd done the right thing. I found myself wondering if we could drive back to Memphis and tell everyone it was all a case of mistaken identity. An Elvis impersonator had broken into Graceland, put on a pair of Elvis's pyjamas and died of excitement in his bathroom. 'You have to think of it as being given a second chance,' I told him at last.

'I did all right with the first one, didn't I?' There were tears pouring down his cheeks.

'You certainly did.'

Eventually, I gave Elvis three Valium tablets and told him they were the strongest sleeping tablets available. I reminded him that he would now be a legend for ever and that his daughter and fans would remember Elvis Presley as he was in his prime and not as he had become in early middle age.

Chapter Eighteen

In recent months Dr Nick had made an attempt to wean Elvis off some of his drugs and had replaced a few of the active pills with placebos, but the King was still probably one of the worst prescription drug addicts in show business – where, in the 1970s, all the really heavy duty prescription drug addicts could be found.

Before we had left Graceland I had promised Elvis two things: first that I would help him lose weight and second that I would help him come off the prescription drugs he was taking. In a way these were non optional.

There was no way that I could get Elvis out of the country unless he lost a good deal of weight. It was the easiest way I could think of to change his appearance dramatically. The newspapers and the television news programmes would help us by constantly showing pictures of Elvis as he had been just before his death – when he was at his heaviest. A slimmed down and lightly disguised Elvis might merit a glance but hopefully no more; I was betting that, at worst, most people would think he just looked like Elvis as he had looked at the beginning of his career. If, very occasionally, someone came up to him and said `You look like a young, slimmer version of Elvis Presley' we would be OK.

And he had to stop taking prescription drugs. As Elvis Presley there had never been any problem in obtaining all the drugs he needed. There were always plenty of doctors happy to write out prescriptions, or dole out bottles full of pills, in return for being able to say that they were treating Elvis Presley. But from now on things would be very different. It would be hard, if not impossible, for us to have such ready access to doctors and drugs.

I had been for some time conscious that it would not be possible for Elvis to take all his pills with him. If his bathroom cabinet didn't contain enough pills to stock a pharmacy then a good many people would be asking questions. And so I had been filching drugs from his collection, and from the general drug store in Graceland, and storing them in my own room. So that he wouldn't complain that his pill supplies were being stolen I told Elvis what I was doing. It had been absurdly easy for him to obtain replacement pills from the doctors, dentists and pharmacists who fed his addiction.

When we left Graceland for the last time I'd put the drugs I'd collected (and which I now hoped would prove to be enough to last us until Elvis kicked his various habits) into the small, undistinguished looking canvas holdall which already contained our new passports and the keys for the apartments in New York and Paris.

The Valium I gave Elvis to help him sleep came from this collection. It was the last time he ever took drugs to help him sleep.

Chapter Nineteen

We stayed in that apartment for three long months. I went out two or three times a week to buy groceries, books, magazines and newspapers but Elvis did not leave the flat at all. The balcony proved to be a life saver. I honestly think that if he hadn't been able to pace up and down outside whenever he wanted to Elvis would have gone stark raving mad. Without the balcony the apartment would have surely seemed like a prison. Our other life saver was the Betamax video player which the owner had left in the apartment. There was a rental shop a block and a half away and I think we went through their entire stock of video films in the first month. We must have watched every cowboy film ever made.

    I had to buy us both clothes, of course, since we had come away with no more than the clothes we stood up in. Buying clothes for Elvis was easy because now that he'd lost weight we were pretty much the same size around the chest and waist. We'd always been the same height to within half an inch or so. I did the clothes shopping at a store which specialised in jackets and trousers which were cut in a rather old-fashioned English style. Elvis was horrified when I returned with a carrier bag containing a tweed sports jacket, two pairs of grey flannels and a dull selection of shirts and ties, socks and underwear. 'Couldn't you have found me a jump suit?' he asked, pulling a face when I gave him the jacket. I also bought him a pair of dark brown brogues which he looked at with particular distaste. Since we were only going to be in New York for three months there was little point in buying more clothes than we were going to need to get us to Paris. We could both replenish our wardrobes when we arrived in France.

    For the first two weeks we spent most of our time sitting watching the news on the television. Slowly, Elvis's death stopped being the only news item but for a while everything else had to take second place. Donald's body was embalmed at the Memphis Funeral Home and returned to Graceland on the 17th August. Vernon had ordered a public viewing of the casket, which I thought was pretty confident of him, if not actually reckless, and this was set up in the foyer at the house. The news programmes said that over 30,000 fans were allowed to file past. To be honest I was surprised it was so few. When a big star dies in France vast crowds, measured in millions, turn out to say 'goodbye'.

All city buildings in Memphis flew their flags at half-mast and President Jimmy Carter ordered 300 National Guard troops into the area to make sure that public order was maintained though the man in the White House never explained just what sort of rioting he expected from thousands of sobbing fans.

The funeral itself took place on the 18th of August in the living room at Graceland. There were surprisingly few celebrities there; just singer James Brown, actor George Hamilton and actress Ann-Margret who had starred in 'Viva Las Vegas' with Elvis. There was no doubt that Elvis was disappointed at the turnout of celebrities. He kept asking why John Wayne and Burt Reynolds weren't there. I told him they were probably keeping away so that the funeral didn't become a media event but I didn't really believe that. If I'd been Elvis I'd have found the turnout disappointing too. A comedian called Jackie Kahane, who often opened Elvis's shows, read a testimonial and a few of the music acts who had worked with Elvis on his stage shows performed some of his favourite hymns. He was touched by that. Finally, Donald's body was placed alongside Elvis's mother in the mausoleum at Forest Hills Cemetery. Elvis was upset that a man he had met only once was being buried next to his mother but I couldn't help thinking how proud Donald would have been. It truly was the ultimate accolade for an Elvis Presley impersonator. (Donald would later be moved to Graceland, after there had been an attempt to steal the body from the Forest Hills Cemetery.)

Gradually, day by day and week by week, we worked our way towards our two main objectives. Elvis's life had changed so dramatically that he did not have as much difficulty in giving up his drug and junk food diet as I had feared. At the end of the first week he had lost seven pounds in weight and during the second week I made him shave off his trademark sideburns – which must have contributed to the following week's loss of six pounds. I bought a few guide books and phrase books and Elvis started to learn a little more about the country where he was going into exile. When there was news about France on the television we watched it with a new and special interest. In September, just a few weeks after Elvis's `death', a man called Hamida Djandoubi, a convicted murderer and rapist, was guillotined in Paris. I don't mind admitting that we were both a little shocked by that. We were used to the idea of criminals being executed because it was, after all, a common enough event in America, but the idea of executing a man by telling him to kneel down underneath the blade of a guillotine seemed curiously old-fashioned.

We talked a good deal about his career. People who didn't know Elvis often thought of him as `just' a singer; a puppet performer who had little or no insight into his success. But that wasn't true. Elvis understood his success better than anyone. He was, without a doubt, the most successful entertainer of his generation and arguably the most successful of all time but he never failed to give fortune her due credit.

`Success comes as a result of a mixture of talent, hard work and luck,' he said one evening. He spoke slowly, picking his words with care. `The successful always underestimate the significance of luck and the unsuccessful always overestimate its importance.' He looked at me and smiled. `I had two really big pieces of luck. The first was being able to sing like a black man at just the right time.'

`And the second?' I asked.

`Meeting the Colonel.'

At the end of three months Elvis had lost 50 pounds of bacon and peanut butter inspired blubber and looked like a new person. He wasn't as slim as he had been at 25 but he wasn't anywhere near as fat as he had been when he'd left Memphis. His hips had reappeared and his face was much thinner. In some respects it had, I suspect, been the most painless weight loss programme ever undertaken. Elvis had lost his appetite for the two weeks after his `death' and when it had returned it had been but a shadow of its former self. His binge eating had, of course, been his way of dealing with the fear. A psychiatrist would have probably argued that he had been overeating in the unspoken hope that he would eventually become too obese to appear on stage at all. Elvis was still under enormous stress, of course. He had to watch his daughter, his fiancée, his father, his long-standing manager, his friends and his fans at his own funeral. That's not something many of us have to endure and it is almost impossible to imagine the pain Elvis felt at that time, and for a long while afterwards. Vernon and the Colonel had known the truth but Lisa Marie and Ginger had not and nor had the mourning friends and employees with whom he had shared so many experiences. Their loss was tangible, their tears were real. Elvis was, inevitably, racked with guilt and I repeatedly had to remind him that if he had stayed at Graceland he would have almost certainly have become a genuine corpse within weeks. I told him I believed that if he had gone on stage one more time he would have probably collapsed and died in the middle of a show.

I thought about disconnecting the television, of course. But although I'm no doctor it did seem to me that it would be healthier for Elvis to deal with the pain of his funeral at the time it was happening, rather than to have to deal with it bit by bit over the years to come. Besides, the imagination is such a powerful force that I have no doubt that the pain of the scenes Elvis would have created in his mind would have probably exceeded the pain of real life, awful though that was.

Within days of the funeral many of the show business commentators on television were concentrating on the sales of Elvis's records and there was much talk about the vast sums being brought in by the vast array of souvenir merchandise that Vernon and the Colonel were promoting with great enthusiasm. It was of some small comfort to Elvis to know that his daughter and his father would be well provided for as a result of his `death'. He knew, as well as anyone except the Colonel, that his expenses had been exceeding his income for years and that if he had lived and not toured there would have had to be severe changes to the lifestyles of those living at Graceland.

Although we were both pleased at the weight loss it was the fact that Elvis had managed to kick his drug habits that really delighted us. Giving up the pills had proved much easier than we had feared.

It was no secret at the time, and it is certainly no secret now, that in order to cope with the stress of life in a goldfish bowl Elvis had become addicted to a variety of prescription drugs. Elvis had never considered himself to be an addict. He regarded drug addicts as people who bought their kicks illegally and then used needles and syringes to access them. And the drugs he took had all been prescribed and supplied by properly qualified professionals. But it would be disingenuous to deny that he had been an addict. Of the drugs he was relied on, and could not function without, I suspect that Demerol and Valium were the two most powerful, and the most difficult to give up taking. At Graceland he took vast quantities of these, and other, drugs and in the way of addicts everywhere eventually required vast quantities in order to function. I know that if I had taken the number of drugs Elvis was taking I would have been unconscious for 24 hours a day. It was the drugs which affected Elvis's memory and which resulted in him forgetting the words to songs he had sung so many times. And with the dependence on drugs came the dependence on people. He relied heavily on Dr Nick and the other health care professionals who had prescribed for him. And he now admits that like all addicts he was not above manipulating circumstances in order to get access to extra drugs. `I faked some toothaches when I wanted more pills,' he told me. `No one can prove you don't have toothache can they?' Criticism, particularly when it came from those who had been close to him, and whom he had trusted, invariably and inevitably resulted in him taking more drugs.

Giving up Demerol, a brand name for a variety of morphine called pethidine, is usually difficult. But Valium, a brand name for diazepam, a benzodiazepine drug and a widely prescribed tranquilliser, is generally accepted to be even more difficult for addicts to live without. Most drug addiction experts now agree that diazepam, and the drugs in the same group, are pretty much the most addictive products on the planet. Millions of people were, and are, hooked on them but very few people have taken the amounts of diazepam that Elvis took. Although they are widely used these drugs are not terribly safe; researchers have shown that they can cause brain damage, memory loss, anxiety and depression. They can also cause aggression, violence and antisocial behaviour. Elvis believes now that much of his behaviour while living at Graceland was influenced by these drugs.

And, of course, like all addictive drugs, benzodiazepines such as diazepam can produce huge problems when the addict tries to give them up. Experts have reported that the side effects endured by people giving up diazepam include: tremors, panic, dizziness, faintness, nausea, an inability to concentrate, headaches, tiredness, poor coordination, sweating, aching muscles, hallucinations, blurred vision and increased sensitivity to noise, light and touch. Those are just some of the withdrawal side effects. The official list is longer.

Elvis suffered from most if not all of these symptoms.

But the big problem most addicts face when giving up these drugs is that they also have to deal with the return of the underlying problems: the reasons why they took the pills in the first place. Diazepam works largely by numbing the senses. The people who take the drug are less aware of the world. They become zombies, sleep walkers, wandering through life with a reduced appreciation of what is happening around them and to them.

And here Elvis did have an advantage.

His life had changed completely. And the problems, anxieties and stresses which had resulted in him needing the drugs in the first place had all gone. He no longer had to worry about performing, about making enough money to meet the enormous cost of running Graceland, meeting his payroll costs and maintaining his image as a superstar. (If you're Elvis Presley you can't go to discount stores to pick up cheap toilet rolls, you can't fly economy class on ordinary airlines and you can't be seen in public wearing scruffy clothes. Your fans expect you to live a certain lifestyle.)

He had new stresses, of course. And there is no denying that the new stresses were huge. He had no real idea what sort of life he was heading for. In his despair and desperation to leave the life he had been living he had trusted me to plan everything relating to his future. He knew we were going to Paris and that he was going to become someone else but he knew nothing more. He didn't even know his new name. But these new stresses were new and un-quantified and I think Elvis was protected from them partly because he was excited about the future and partly because he was relieved to have left behind a life that had given him everything a man could wish for, only for him to find that the price he had to pay was unbearably high. In some ways I think that at that point I was suffering almost as much stress as Elvis. I was very well aware of the responsibility I had taken on. Sometimes I lay awake at night, endlessly questioning the decisions I had made.

Chapter Twenty

After we had been in the New York apartment for three months I told Elvis that I thought we were ready to leave the United States of America. He had lost a vast amount of weight and had removed his sideburns. I had cut his hair with specialist scissors and clippers I'd bought and he now had an even more extreme haircut than the one when he'd been a soldier in Germany. He had also managed to grow a particularly luxuriant moustache.

I explained that we were going to drive north to the Canadian border and cross over at Niagara Falls. We would then sell my car to a dealer in Canada and take a train to the airport from which we were going to fly to Europe. I explained that that two of us would fly to Europe on the same flight but that we would be travelling separately. 'If anyone sees you and thinks you look like Elvis Presley they'll assume that you're just a bloke who looks a bit like Elvis,' I explained. 'No one will expect to see Elvis Presley travelling alone on a commercial flight.'

'I want you to wear these,' I told him, giving him a box containing a pair of brown contact lenses. 'And these,' I added, handing him a pair of tortoiseshell spectacles which were fitted with very low powered magnifying lenses. They were almost plain glass, but not quite. I could only imagine that the previous owner had bought them for their cosmetic appeal rather than as a visual aid. I'd picked them up from a street vendor in London who'd had a large cardboard box full of pairs of spectacles. People who needed glasses but couldn't afford to visit an optician plucked spectacles from the box, tried them on, eventually found a pair that suited them and bought them for a couple of pounds. I'd been surprised to see the citizens of England, the home of socialised medicine, reduced to such methods but for me it was a convenient way to purchase spectacles without having to create a paper record. The glasses I had chosen for Elvis had a rather old-fashioned, academic sort of air and I thought they went rather well with the sports jacket, grey flannel trousers and brown brogues. He looked like a fairly young old fogie; a junior university professor, perhaps.

'Why am I wearing spectacles as well as contact lenses?' asked Elvis.

'The contact lenses change the colour of your eyes and the spectacles change the shape of your face. Besides no one will suspect that you're wearing contact lenses if you're wearing spectacles.'

Since Elvis had been indoors for three months I decided that before we set off for Niagara Falls we should go for a walk around the city; just to get him used to being amongst people who didn't drool at his approach and faint when he drew close. So at lunchtime on the day before we were due to drive up to Canada he put on his spectacles, his new jacket and brogues and added a flat cap I'd purchased for him. He carried a well-worn but expensive looking leather briefcase I'd purchased from a second hand luggage store.

We walked for thirty minutes without anyone taking any notice. At lunchtime everyone in New York is going somewhere in a hurry. They're rushing out to grab some lunch or they're rushing back to the office or they're rushing to go to the bank or do some shopping. Wherever they are going they are rushing. Elvis bought some magazines and a newspaper and we both bought a couple of books for our flight to Europe. We also bought two small suitcases, one each, in which to carry our meagre belongings. Since neither of us had credit cards we had to pay cash for everything. All our expenses for the last three months had come out of the $100,000 Vernon Presley had given us. The $20,000 the Colonel had given me when I'd gone to Europe to obtain the passports and rent the two apartments had long ago run out. We had enough money to buy our airline tickets and to keep us alive for a while in Paris before I needed to start turning some of the diamonds into cash. Once we got to Paris we needed to open bank accounts and obtain credit cards but in those days there was no real nonsense about proving who you were; you could open a bank account with a letter from your mum and two old bus tickets. And we both had perfectly legal passports in our new names.

We were on our way back to the apartment when a couple in their mid twenties approached us. They looked like out-of-towners enjoying a break to New York. He wore a poplin golfing jacket which looked totally out of place in the city and she was wearing a knee length beige raincoat. He had one of those little rucksacks on his back and she was carrying a handbag big enough to hold a week's groceries for a family of six. My heart felt as though it were about to jump out of my chest and Elvis's must have been doing the same. I was certain they'd recognised Elvis.

'Excuse me,' said the man. He looked at Elvis first and then at me. At that moment I remember thinking that even if they thought Elvis looked like Elvis they wouldn't expect him to be walking along a street in New York. Plus, the last pictures everyone had seen of Elvis had shown him looking very fat.

'What do you want?' I asked him rather brusquely, my terseness inspired by a fear that he was about to ask Elvis if he'd mind posing for a photograph. I suddenly realised how cold it was and wondered what the devil we were doing walking about in New York on a cold wintry day without coats.

'We're a bit lost,' said the man. 'I know we should have bought a map. But can you tell us the way to Bloomingdale's Department Store?'

'I doubt if we can afford to buy anything there,' said the woman, rather apologetically. 'But we just wanted to take a look around.'

Elvis didn't have a clue, of course, but as luck had it I knew where the store was. I gave them directions. They thanked us and walked away.

'I think I probably died again,' said Elvis. He sounded hoarse, as though his throat had dried.

'You and me both,' I replied. I couldn't have been more drained if I'd just been interrogated in front of a Grand Jury. When Elvis had spoken I had been terrified. I had suddenly realised that his voice was, of course, just as much of a giveaway as his sideburns had been.

It was only later that I remembered that people don't usually see what they don't expect to see. And why would anyone visiting New York in search of a Bloomingdale shopping experience expect to see the King of Rock'n'Roll, recently deceased, walking around with a chum.

We went back to our leased apartment stopping only to buy a pack of six doughnuts. There is a time when junk food is the only thing that will do.

I spent the rest of the day trying to teach Elvis to speak with a little less of a drawl, and teaching him to use English words such as 'bonnet', 'braces' and 'trousers' instead of 'hood', 'suspenders' and 'pants'.

'Suspenders are the little strappy things women use to hold up their stockings,' I told him, much to his astonishment. 'And pants are the flimsy items of lingerie they wear under their dresses. If you tell people you're wearing pants and suspenders they'll think you're a crossdresser.'

Elvis laughed at this. It was the first time I'd heard him laugh for quite a while. Heaven knows, he hadn't had much to laugh at. His eyes always lit up when he was amused. I realised, for the first time, that whatever name he used, and whatever disguise he wore there was nothing at all I could do to protect the female inhabitants of Paris from the charm and the charismatic smile. Even without the looks, the voice and the Colonel, Elvis would have been a star. He was a man born to be King.

'The 'sidewalk' is the 'pavement', a 'trailer' is a 'caravan' and 'gasoline' is known as 'petrol',' I added. This produced more laughter. 'A 'yard' is a 'garden', 'chips' are 'crisps',' I warned him. 'And you must never, ever use the word 'fanny' in public.'

It occurred to me that teaching Elvis to speak English like a native of London or Liverpool was probably going to be as hard as helping him to learn French. It was probably a good thing that we were going to live as Englishmen in France, rather than in England.

Chapter Twenty One

That evening I gave Elvis his new passport.

It now seems difficult to believe but although we had been living in the apartment in New York for three months Elvis had never once shown any interest in his new identity.

Because he hadn't spoken to anyone except me there really hadn't been any need to call him anything other than Elvis. And although I don't claim to have any understanding of human psychology it did seem to me that I should let Elvis retain his name for as long as possible. He had already given up everything else he had of his first life.

I had our two new passports (and the birth certificates with which we had obtained them) in my bag, along with the keys for the Paris apartment I had rented and the diamonds Vernon had given me to safeguard Elvis's future. I took the passports out of the bag, checked that I was giving him the correct one, and handed Elvis his new identity.

These new passports would be the keys which would open our new world. With them, and the new identities they gave us, we could start afresh; we could open genuine bank accounts, acquire credit cards, buy property and find jobs.

Elvis opened his new passport, flicked through it until he found the page with his photograph on and stared at what he saw in voiceless disbelief.

`This is my new name?'

`Yes.'

`This is who I'm going to be?' Elvis looked at me.

`Yes.'

`I've got to live with this name for the rest of my life?'

`Yes. Unless we find a new gravestone and start again.'

Elvis threw the passport down on the table. `You couldn't find anything better than that?'

'I had to find babies who were born and died in the 1930's. People in England sometimes gave their children funny names back then.'

Elvis reached out and picked up the passport. He opened it and looked at it, as though hoping that the name in it might have changed. It hadn't. He closed the passport and put it back down on the table.

'I didn't think you'd want to be Cedric, Bruce or Cyril. Those were the only other names I could find.'

'Couldn't you have found me a `Tom', `Dick' or `Harry'?'

'There weren't any I'm afraid.'

'What's your new name?'

I showed him my passport.

Elvis laughed. 'That's even worse than mine.' He put my new passport down on the table beside his own.

'I gave you the best name.'

Elvis looked at me and raised an eyebrow. 'The best?'

'The best of the two. The best I could find.'

'If you ever, ever call me by that name I'll kill you. Even if I have to do it with my bare hands.' He put his hands in a circle, as though strangling me.

'OK.'

Neither of us spoke for a while.

'I'll have to call you something in public. I can't call you Elvis.'

Elvis thought for a while. Then he smiled. Then he laughed. 'In private you can call me Jesse. If we're with other people you can call me the damned name on that darned passport.'

Just before we went to bed I burnt my own original passport, the one in my real name. It felt strange and for a few moments I got close to understanding the feelings Elvis must have experienced. I now had nothing to connect me to my past. At least Elvis still had his voice, his charisma and his memories. As far as the world was concerned the voice would be silent and the memories private but the charisma would never desert him.

We had both put our past into boxes, sealed them, locked them and buried them out of sight. Now all we had was a future.

Chapter Twenty Two

The drive up to Canada and the flight across the Atlantic went without a hitch. In fact, everything went so smoothly that I thought of Bernard Shaw's play `Pygmalion' and the scene in which Professor Higgins watches his protégé, Eliza Doolittle, wow the aristocracy. Higgins enjoys watching Nepommuck, the linguist and interpreter, listen to Eliza's accent, looking for signs that she is a fake. And I almost shared the Professor's unspoken wish that something would happen to alleviate the tedium. Maybe a fan would recognise Elvis's profile. Maybe a stewardess would feel a tingle in her neck when he spoke. But the word `almost' was always there; written in red ink and in capital letters.

The flight wasn't much fun and we were both glad when it was over. To avoid drawing any attention to ourselves we had seats at the back of the plane. I'm told that these days the legroom is barely adequate and the food barely edible but just a few decades ago, there seemed to be plenty of room and the food had been prepared with thought and was served with smiles. We shared a row of seats with an old woman who fell asleep as soon as we took off and didn't stop snoring until the plane landed. Elvis sat next to her and didn't mind a bit; a sleeping old lady wasn't likely to stare at him for hour after hour before announcing: `I know who you are!'

In Dublin we spent a night in a pleasant old hotel in the city centre before flying on to Paris. With the benefit of hindsight I don't know why I complicated our journey with this stopover in Ireland. I suppose I was thinking that if anyone traced our journey across the Atlantic, they might lose our trail in Dublin. All I can say is that it must have seemed a good idea at the time and it did give Elvis a chance to discover that he didn't much like the taste of draught Guinness and to buy a tweed cap and a shillelagh from a small shop in the hotel. When I left him in the corridor outside his room that evening I saw that he was struggling to hold back tears.

`When I saw the racks of postcards in the shop downstairs I wanted to send cards to Lisa Marie, and Ginger and the guys at

Graceland,' he said, sadly. 'But then I realised that I couldn't. And that there isn't anyone in the world I can write to anymore.'

I nodded. I understood what he meant. Elvis was now the only person in the world I knew. But he had given up so much more than I had.

We flew together from Ireland to Paris, buying our return tickets with cash. I changed some dollars into French francs at the airport and then took a taxi from the airport to our apartment in the 15th arrondissement. The flight and the journey through two customs posts were uneventful. Border guards had not yet become drunk on their pinch of power and it was perfectly possible to travel from country to country without feeling like a criminal.

'Why are we buying return tickets?' Elvis had asked, puzzled. 'Are we coming back to Ireland?'

'We're not coming back - certainly not with these tickets. But if anyone manages to trace us this far they'll probably assume we did.'

'So they won't start looking for us in Paris?'

'That's the idea!'

We had nearly three months left on our rental agreement for the flat and I already had the keys in my pocket. I was relieved when Elvis nodded his approval. It was, it seemed, just the sort of place he'd expected. He particularly liked the fact that there was a 'what to do in an emergency' card pinned to the wall in the hallway outside our apartment and that the card contained just one line of advice: 'Gardez Votre Sang-Froid'.

'What's that mean?' asked Elvis.

'Keep your self-control.'

'That's it? That's the emergency advice?'

'Yes. The French would rather die in style than show signs of panic and have to be saved without looking cool.' I told him that I'd heard of a French woman whose apartment building was on fire who had refused to allow the fireman to carry her down the ladder until she'd finished putting on her make-up and choosing a suitably modest dress for the journey.

The apartment, which had lain empty for a few months, was freezing cold so we turned the heating full on, dumped our bags and headed out to find a café where we could have a meal and a shop where we could pick up bread, milk and a few other essentials.

Before we left the apartment I emptied the diamonds Vernon Presley had given us and poured them into the bottom of the ice tray in the refrigerator. I then added water and put the tray back in the freezer compartment. 'You can't have drinks with ice in them,' I told Elvis. 'If you put an ice cube into a glass it will be the most expensive drink you've ever had.' I hoped that the diamonds wouldn't need to be there for long. My plan was to turn the stones into cash as soon as I could find a reputable dealer and then slowly feed the cash into a new bank account in Elvis's name. There was slightly more than $70,000 left of the $100,000 which Vernon had handed me and I thought that ought to be enough to keep Elvis going for quite a while – particularly since his expenses would now be considerably lower.

I had to find a job.

Chapter Twenty Three

Now that we were in Paris there was much that we needed to do. I had to find myself that job, of course, but I also needed to help Elvis find something to do with his days. He had spent two decades working, rehearsing or worrying about his next show. With nearly $2 million in diamonds sitting in the ice making compartment of our refrigerator I sincerely hoped and believed that he wouldn't have to worry about earning enough money to live on, but I knew darned well that he wouldn't be content to spend the rest of his life sitting in Parisian parks, sticking stamps in an album or crocheting antimacassars. We needed to find a new apartment (or, possibly, two apartments). The diamonds had to be turned into cash and the cash put somewhere safe where it could earn its living. And we both had to obtain cartes de sejour; the official papers which would enable us to live and work in Paris as residents.

But we both decided that we deserved a few days rest before we did any of these things. Since neither of us had done very much for three months or so it may seem strange to say that we needed a rest, but the stresses and strains of those months had taken its toll. I was waking up every night worrying that I might have done, or not done, something that would result in a television crew from somewhere in America appearing on our doorstep one evening. And Elvis had become prone to occasional but worryingly lengthy bouts of depression. He would sit with a book or magazine in his hand, as though reading, but it would be perfectly clear that he wasn't reading at all. He would sit and stare into space and the pages wouldn't move. From time to time he was terse and sharp, and I suspected that he sometimes felt that he had been weak to run away from a life he could no longer bear. I knew, because we had talked about it, that he felt his fans could never possibly understand why he'd done what he did. And he never said as much but I suspected that he sometimes blamed me for the fact that he was now living in a flat in Paris, rather than playing the part of Lord of the Manor at Graceland. We agreed that before we made plans for our new lives we both needed a little time to get our breath and to accustom ourselves to the world we'd chosen for our future.

Besides, we had to learn our way around our arrondissement. And while I needed to rediscover the Paris I had once known well Elvis needed to learn the Paris he'd never really known at all. His previous visits to Paris had always involved hotels, nightclubs and girls. Now he needed to find out where to buy the best bread, how to deal with French waiters and where best to purchase English language books and newspapers. I could help Elvis with some of these things but I needed to take a refresher course in Paris life. The streets and main buildings may stay the same (and this is probably truer of Paris, where almost every building is a national monument, than most towns and cities in Europe and almost all towns and cities in America) but cities have lives of their own and are forever changing in subtle and sometimes hardly unnoticeable ways. The times of Metro trains change and bus routes are revised. Shops and restaurants go in and out of fashion. Habits and courtesies are adjusted as people adapt their lives to new demands and new expectations.

When he had been living at Graceland, Elvis had kept what most people would have probably regarded as unusual hours. He rarely got up before lunchtime and often had breakfast in the middle or late afternoon. When you're a true superstar, and you live in your own tailor-made environment, surrounded by people who exist only to pamper and obey, then the rules are what you say they are. And, gradually, over the years, Elvis had created for himself a lifestyle that could comfortably be described as eccentric. The Colonel, who spent most of his time away from Graceland, and much of it sitting at gambling tables, didn't care a fig how Elvis lived as long as he was available to get the cash registers ringing whenever required.

In New York, inspired partly by the lifestyle of our neighbours and the daytime noise of the traffic, Elvis had gradually changed his body clock so that he arose at a more usual and convenient hour and by the time we moved to Paris he was accustomed to having his breakfast at around 10.00 am. This would, I suspect, have been quite a surprise to the people who'd known him at Graceland. But then a good many things about the new Elvis would have surprised the inhabitants of Graceland.

And so, on our first morning in Paris, we hit the streets at a few minutes before 11.00 am. If the old Elvis had been awake at this time it would have been because he hadn't yet gone to bed. It was one of those crisp, winter mornings that Paris does so well. The air was cold but the sky was as blue as it would have been on a bright, summer's day. We both agreed that the first very thing we had to do was to buy ourselves decent winter coats and scarves. In Paris, everyone wears scarves. And the inhabitants of that great city would no more dream of going out onto the cold streets without their overcoats in winter than they would dream of venturing onto the beach wearing socks. We'd managed without coats in New York, even though the weather had been just as cold, but we were definitely going to need coats if we were going to survive in Paris.

One of the beauties of the City of Light is that, unlike many cities around the world, it is a place that is lived in. It is, and always has been, a city for dwelling rather than a city for business and the city's politicians have always taken seriously their responsibility to the people who actually live in the city as well as those who visit as tourists or to trade. Paris was originally given the soubriquet 'City of Light' because it was a centre of ideas and education during the Age of Enlightenment, but in recent years the title has had a more practical explanation. In 1828, to make life easier for the city's thousands of flaneurs, Paris lit the Champs Élysées with gas lamps and became, quite literally, La Ville-Lumiere; the City of Light.

Very few people actually live in the centre of London and so the vast majority of the shops cater not for locals but for visitors. London is a city designed for businessmen, tourists and shoppers who've come up to town for the day to look at the frocks in Oxford Street or to walk around Harrods and marvel at the prices. Paris is different. Unlike Londoners, who tend to live in suburbs an hour's crowded, dirty and uncomfortable ride out from the city centre, Parisians tend to live in the heart of their city; often within walking distance of the building where they work. There are schools, nurseries and supermarkets scattered throughout the city and every arrondissement in Paris is a village with its own mayor, television repair man and picture framer. Each arrondissement has a character of its own and although the areas which contain the biggest attractions (such as the Eiffel Tower, Sacre Coeur, Notre Dame and so on) are blessed with the usual shops selling T-shirts, berets and key rings, there are also plenty of shops catering for the residents and selling vacuum cleaners, olive oil and winter coats.

We bought our winter coats (light grey for Elvis and dark blue for me) from a genial young shop assistant who didn't seem at all surprised that we had found ourselves in Paris in the middle of winter wearing nothing warmer than sports jackets and flannels. He fussed, made sure the coats fitted us and then, after he had handed us the bill but before we had paid it, asked us for our initials and then begged us to wait for a few moments. He took the coats, disappeared into a backroom and returned a few minutes later to show us that the coats had our initials neatly embroidered into the silk lining just beneath the collar.

'Dans le case ou il ya confusion dans un restaurant,' he said.

Elvis looked at me, waiting for a translation. 'They've put our initials into the coats in case we're in a restaurant and there is confusion about the ownership of a coat.'

Elvis, who had never heard of such a thing, thought this was absolutely brilliant.

We paid and then Elvis remembered that we wanted scarves as well. We both chose woollen ones. Elvis picked one in maroon and I selected a grey one. Elvis insisted that the assistant had our initials embroidered on the scarves. The assistant thought this a splendid idea and was so delighted that he gave us a short course in how to tie a scarf the Parisian way.

I confess I'd never thought about this before. I'd always regarded a scarf as something one draped around one's neck, or tied as though one was tying a necktie and had got bored and given up half way through. But the shop assistant showed us how to fold the scarf in two, drape the doubled scarf around our necks and then poke the loose ends through the loop.

We left feeling very proud of ourselves. And, since we were wearing coats tailored in France, neatly augmented by French woollen scarves tied in the fashionable Parisian way, we rather thought we fitted in, and looked for all the world like a couple of Frenchmen wandering about the city, on our way to some important business appointment, but with time to spare to enjoy the sights and sounds that surrounded us. Very French, very Parisian.

Chapter Twenty Four

At a small bookshop, still in the 15th arrondissement, we purchased two guide books (in English), a phrase book for Elvis, two French-English dictionaries and two maps of the city. Most hotels and even a good many cafés give away free maps (usually paid for by department stores which add, for the traveller's convenience, a large arrow drawing attention to the location of the sponsoring establishment) but I felt we needed something a little more comprehensive. The bookseller, who spoke excellent English, told us that the small, red map books which he sold us were particularly popular with Parisians themselves. The map books also contained Autobus and Metro route maps and we both still own the ones we bought that day. They were the most useful things we ever bought. The bus and subway routes and time tables have long since become out-of-date but rues, avenues and boulevards don't often change their names and so the meatier parts of the two books have remained invaluable.

We had our lunch in a café from which we had an excellent view of the Eiffel Tower. Elvis, I remember, had a burger with fries but without cheese and I introduced him to the joy of drinking vin chaud.

Vin chaud (hot wine) is one of the best kept secrets of winter in Paris. Every café in the city will serve it but very few bother to include it on their menu or wine list. The drink originated in Paris in the 17th century. Customers at Francesco Procopio dei Costelli's establishment, underneath the arches around the Jardin du Palais Royale, could purchase a drink called hippocras – a glass of sweet wine spiced with cinnamon, ginger, cloves and mace. Today the drink consists, as the name suggests, of hot red wine served in a glass with a slice of orange or lemon added. The customer then adds cinnamon and sugar to suit his own palate.

In his previous life, Elvis rarely drank alcohol and he was suspicious at first but it didn't take him long to be converted and, like most converts, to become enthusiastic. It's a taste that has never left him. Today, if you were to spot Elvis sitting in one of his favourite cafés between the months of November and March the chances are better than good that he will have a glass of vin chaud in front of him and one inside him. On that, our first day of our new lives, we each had another vin chaud before we headed back out onto the pavement.

'How long do these people have for lunch?' asked Elvis, as we left the café. 'There are guys in there who were eating when we arrived.'

I explained to him that the French believe in lengthy lunches. They like to give themselves time to enjoy their food and wine and they like to give their stomachs time to digest what they have eaten. Since a light lunch for a Frenchman is a bottle of red wine and an omelette made with half a dozen eggs and a quarter of a pound of cheese this is probably wise. Before lunch there will be a Pernod. After lunch there will be a cognac and an espresso. At that time, in the 1970's, the majority of the French had still not recognised that alcohol could be dangerous. Even the French Government seemed a little uncertain. There used to be an official Government poster on the Metro which read: 'Jamais plus de deux litres par jour'. No more than two litres a day! There was another poster which warned: 'L'alcool tue lentement'. Alcohol kills you slowly. I remember this one particularly because some wag had wandered around the whole of the Metro and added, underneath, these words: 'Tant mieux. Nous ne sommes pas presse'. Fine. We are not in a hurry.

When they've eaten, they chat a little, exchange gossip with the waiter, read the paper and perhaps play a little cards. An elderly Parisian once told me that the French take two hours for lunch because that is the length of time it takes a horse to have a proper feed.

Since we had spent much of the last hour looking at it, we wandered across the Champs de Mars to the Eiffel Tower and gazed up at it in the way everyone does, whether they're seeing it for the first or the hundredth time. Until 1930 the Tower (which deserves the capital initial letter as much as any structure) was the tallest man-made erection in the world and, despite the efforts of some very determined and ambitious architects, it is still the most striking by far and, without a doubt, the most instantly recognisable man-made structure in the world. Monsieur Eiffel, the engineer who designed the Tower that bears his name, and was responsible for building it, used to have a small flat at the very top and that's probably why he installed the lifts. From our guide books we learned that the Tower was built for the 1889 Paris Exhibition, just to show it could be done, and as a rather grand sample book for a man who was primarily a bridge builder. The original plan was to demolish it when the lease on the land ran out in 1909. But, fortunately for Paris, France and the sellers of postcards the Tower turned out to be useful for sending radio communications around Europe and so it escaped the indignity of being turned into the world's biggest scrapyard consignment. Since then the Tower has found many different uses. During the First World War, the French put trained parrots onto the Tower in the hope that they would give advance warning of incoming aircraft, and enable anti-aircraft gunners to shoot down the enemy planes. Sadly, the plan had to be abandoned when the French discovered that the parrots couldn't discriminate between Allied aircraft and German aircraft and that there was, consequently, a real risk that over-eager gunners would shoot down the 11.44 from Marseilles instead of the 11.45 from Berlin. In the years between the two Great wars the Tower was frequently sold by confidence tricksters. One bright fellow made a terribly good living out of repeatedly selling it as scrap metal to a series of gullible American tourists. The conman, who had an accomplice who worked in a French ministry building, would take his marks to an office there to have their wallets professionally lightened. What a wonderfully romantic place the Tower is.

    Then, as now, the area around and underneath the Tower was crowded with tinkers, con artists and wandering salesmen determined to sell you souvenirs you never knew you needed and won't know what to do with when you get them home. Just how many people really want key rings connected to small, cheaply made metal models of the Eiffel Tower? It was also home for a number of artists who had fled that overcrowded market place, La Place du Tetre in Montmartre. (The Place du Tetre, which sits next to Sacre Coeur, right at the top of Montmartre, is the traditional home for street artists but it has been rather overcrowded for some years and those who are elbowed out usually find their way to other tourist haunts such as the area beneath and around the Eiffel Tower.)

We stopped to admire the work of one young artist. He was perched on a collapsible stool using a stick of charcoal to sketch a young girl who was sitting opposite him. She was also perched on a stool, with her boyfriend, fiancé or husband standing behind her keeping a careful eye on the proceedings. These artists prefer collapsible stools because it is easier to pick them up and run with them if a policeman appears on the horizon.

Next to the two stools the artist had lain out on the ground three charcoal sketches of famous people. There was one of Charlie Chaplin, one of General de Gaulle, the former French President, and one of Elvis Presley. They were all good likenesses and Elvis and I weren't the only people standing watching the artist, and admiring his work.

'The drawing of Elvis is brilliant,' said a female American voice.

I looked across at her and knew that Elvis had also noticed her. She was dressed in the universal outfit favoured by all American tourists in those days: jeans, T-shirt, thick anorak and woolly hat. She had a rucksack on her back. Her bearded companion wore similar clothes and also wore a rucksack.

'It's the best likeness,' agreed the young man. 'It was awful that he died so young.' Like the girl he looked to be about twenty years old.

'I cried for a week,' confessed the girl. 'He was fantastic.'

'I've got all his albums,' said the traveller with the beard. It was a rather scruffy beard that needed some work with the scissors.

The two young Americans appeared not to know each other all that well. I guessed they had probably joined up somewhere on their travels around Europe.

'He died at the right time,' said the girl.

I didn't look at him, and there was at least a couple of feet of clear air between us, but I swear that I felt Elvis stiffen.

'He'll always be the King,' said the youth. 'But dying was the best career move. He'd have become a joke if he'd carried on. He'd have ended up doing small clubs for peanuts.'

'They shouldn't have let him do those shows when he'd put on weight,' said the girl. 'I'm glad he didn't do any more.'

'I'll always miss him. He was the best.'

They wandered away, hand in hand, both deep in private thought.

Neither Elvis nor I spoke but we too walked away, heading rather aimlessly towards the river Seine.

We walked for a while and then crossed the river by the Pont d'Alma, just above the spot where, two decades later, Princess Diana would die in a horrific car crash. There is no better way to see Paris than to walk through it. Pedestrians see all sorts of things which are lost to those who travel by taxi, bus or metro. The French even have a special word for a person who wanders through Paris on foot. They call him or her a 'flaneur' – someone who strolls, saunters or wanders the streets at random, aimlessly searching for experiences rather than heading somewhere in particular.

Although we'd been walking for twenty minutes or so we still hadn't exchanged a single word.

'Did you hear that?' asked Elvis suddenly.

I knew exactly to what he was referring. 'Yes. I heard.'

'It was good to hear what they said.' His voice was cracked with emotion.

'I know.'

'I did the right thing, didn't I?'

'I think you did.' I paused. 'You had no choice. I think they were right. The Colonel would have never let you retire. You'd have felt more and more under pressure. The press would have been nastier and nastier. It was all getting out of control.'

Elvis put his arm around my shoulders. I turned and looked at him. He was crying. 'I've been angry with you for a while,' he admitted. 'Angry with you, me, everyone.'

I nodded but didn't speak.

'It was something that had to be done,' he said.

I still didn't say anything. There didn't seem to be any need to say anything.

'But it wasn't easy. The funeral. Watching Lisa Marie. All those weeping fans. Knowing that Graceland is still there. Knowing that daddy and the Colonel are still selling records, little teddy bears and souvenir postcards. Knowing that part of me is dead but, in a strange sort of way, still alive.'

'No one else will ever know what you've been through,' I said softly. There wasn't any point in telling him that I understood because how could anyone possibly understand what pain he'd been through?

'I think I'll be OK now.'

And I think he was. That overheard conversation was a turning point for Elvis. I honestly don't think Elvis ever again felt any doubt that he had done the right thing.

That young couple never knew just important those few words turned out to be. I often wish I could find them and tell them just how much they helped their King.

Maybe they'll read this. And maybe they'll remember.

Chapter Twenty Five

From the Pont d'Alma we wandered along the banks of the Seine. Most visitors to Paris never walk along the banks of the river, though it is a popular pastime with Parisians, particularly on Sundays. On warm days they go down the steps and walk along the bank of the river. They take a book and sit on a bench and watch the river and the ducks drift by. We walked until we reached Pont Alexander III where we turned right and walked up towards the Hotel Des Invalides which, in spite of its name isn't a hotel at all.

This wonderfully impressive building, topped with a dome covered in gold leaf which shines brightly whenever there is any sun, was built as a hospital for wounded soldiers and is now largely occupied by a military museum, though there is still a hospital and a retirement home for war veterans there. However, visitors flock to the Hotel Des Invalides not because of the museum or the hospital but because Napoleon Bonaparte is buried in the crypt of the church, the Chapelle Saint-Jerome.

Elvis and I paid our admission fees and followed the crowd of visitors inspecting the French emperor's final resting place. Neither of us said anything but I couldn't help wondering whether the crowds queuing to visit Graceland were bigger than the crowds at Napoleon's tomb. Would people still be visiting Graceland a century and a quarter after Elvis's official death? And I thought again of Donald, the Elvis impersonator, and I couldn't help smiling to myself. There would, I suspected, be many more Elvis impersonators over the years but could there, would there, ever be an impersonator quite so successful? Of course not. Donald had that particular competition completely sewn up for eternity.

After we'd completed our tour around the dead Emperor's tomb we wandered into the Musee de l'Armee where Elvis, who loves guns, was fascinated to see the length of some of the early rifles which were used by French armies. The theory was that a gun with a very long barrel would be more accurate than a gun with a merely long barrel and so guns were built with barrels so long that one unfortunate soldier had to stand at the business end and hold the gun up in the air while a `marksman' standing several yards away pulled the trigger. When we came out of the museum we wandered around the first floor cloisters which surround the main cobbled courtyard of the Hotel des Invalides. The place was designed so that wounded soldiers could shuffle around the cloisters and take their daily constitutions whatever the weather. The steps up to the first floor cloisters are shallow and wide to make it easier for wounded, one-legged soldiers to climb up and down. Upstairs, the small, solid wooden doors on the cloistered landings open into the small rooms in which the wounded soldiers lived out their final days. It isn't difficult to imagine Napoleon's old guard hobbling around, chatting about the snows of Moscow and delighting in stories of their hero's triumphant return from Elba. Carved in the stone pillars you can still see bits of very early graffiti dating back to the 18th century. At the southern end of the courtyard, above the soldiers' church wherein lies Napoleon's remains, stands a huge statue of Napoleon, gazing out on his imaginary troops and listening to the clatter of skidding hooves on the courtyard cobbles.

We each drank a vin chaud in a pleasantly old-fashioned café across the road and then walked slowly down the Avenue de la Bourdonnais towards the Eiffel Tower. Monsieur Eiffel's magnificent feat of engineering dominates Paris so successfully that it is perfectly possible to find your way around the city simply by using the Tower as a point of reference. If you become lost then you just look up and find the Tower somewhere on the horizon. We bought a bundle of American and British newspapers and magazines from a kiosk on the corner of the Avenue de la Motte-Picquet and purchased an armful of fruit and vegetables from a greengrocery store in the Rue Cler.

`This seems like a good area to live,' said Elvis, studying his map as we walked back down towards the river again `There are loads of fine looking cafés and plenty of small shops.' He looked around and smiled approvingly. I had to remind myself that he was pretty well seeing Paris for the first time. His previous visits had all involved fast limousine rides between hotels and night clubs. He hadn't seen anything much that hadn't been wearing a sequin encrusted G string and a pair of sparkling pasties.

'Let's have a look at the rest of Paris first,' I suggested. 'There's no rush. We've got the apartment we're in for a few more weeks.'

We crossed the road again and wandered into a restaurant that specialised in pizzas. Crossing the road in Paris is always an adventure and on this occasion we both narrowly missed being mown down by a Mercedes taxi which was practising for the French Grand Prix. Taxi drivers in Paris, who are rumoured to be trained on dodgem cars in an unused fairground at a secret location, tend to assume that they are the only people on the planet who matter a jot. They are, moreover, the original multi-taskers, far too talented to waste their days merely driving taxis. The one who nearly ran us over was drinking a cup of coffee and carrying on a heated conversation with the passenger in the back of his cab. Mind you, they aren't always as bright as they like to think they are. I was once in a taxi which collided with a motor cycle. The irate taxi driver (who had been studying his map at the time) leapt out of his taxi and punched the motorcyclist in the face. It was a good blow, delivered accurately and with considerable force. The only problem was that the motorcyclist was still wearing his helmet. The taxi driver was in so much pain that he had to totter into a nearby café and order a medicinal brandy. (In France the words 'medicinal brandy' are code for a triple.)

'Why don't you ever bother using the pedestrian crossings?' asked Elvis. 'There was one just a few yards up the road.'

I laughed and explained that it was a common mistake among visitors to the city to assume that the white strips of paint which cross the road at various points are safe crossing points. The curious idea of allowing pedestrians to cross roads in safety was introduced by the Germans when they invaded Paris during the Second World War. The Germans, a neat and tidy people, were appalled at the way the French just wandered across the roads whenever the fancy took them and so they introduced the idea of pedestrian crossings, marked with the traditional white stripes painted across the road. Unfortunately, the French have never liked being told what to do and they particularly disliked being told what to do by Germans whom they regard as bullet-headed bullies with no sense of style, no sense of taste, an appalling affection for dumplings and a childish sense of humour. The result is that pedestrians ignore the crossings and motorists treat them with utter disdain; often making them unusable by parking right across them. Even the fact that a French Government passed a law making motorists legally responsible for the damage they cause when they run over pedestrians who are using these crossings made no difference to the way they are regarded.

We sat in the pizza restaurant for an hour waiting to be served.

'It's a damned good looking city,' said Elvis.

I agreed with him and explained that Paris was re-designed, and largely rebuilt, in the 19th century under the influence of a civic planner called Georges-Eugene Haussmann (known to the common or garden builders and labourers who did the actual work as the Baron Haussmann) who was hired by Napoleon III to modernise Paris. Haussmann had several aims. He wanted to create a city with safer, brighter, more open streets, friendlier communities and more space for traffic. He also wanted avenues so broad that French rebels would find it difficult to build barricades across them and he built broad avenues between the main railway stations so that troops could be brought in from the provinces to quell any uprisings. Old, crumbling, filthy apartment houses were pulled down and replaced with smart new buildings which had uniform heights and gave the city a unique elegance. Elvis was impressed when I told him that a century or so later Haussmann's Paris was still regarded as a blueprint for good city planning and that his design had, over the years, been followed by planners in dozens of other major cities around the world. 'At the time the citizens of Paris weren't all enthusiastic,' I told him. 'When they realised that Haussmann had spent 2.5 billion francs on rebuilding the city they forced Napoleon III to fire him.'

'Well I think he did a good job. They should name a street after him,' said Elvis.

'They have,' I told him. 'The Boulevard Haussmann is one of the main streets in Paris. It's busy, noisy and scruffy these days. This is the area where the rich, powerful and posh tend to live. I suspect you're right and that we'll end up living around here somewhere.'

I explained that Paris is divided into twenty arrondissements, or villages, that each arrondissement tends to have its own character and style, and that the 7th Arrondissement, where the Eiffel Tower is situated, is one of the most expensive areas of the city.

Eventually, tired of waiting for a waiter to serve us, and having noticed that the café also provided a delivery service, I got up from our table and walked across to the pay telephone. It was, as these things usually are in French cafés, next to the toilets. I telephoned the café's own number and ordered two pizzas, giving the woman who answered the telephone the café's own address. Shortly after I had walked back to our table and explained to Elvis what I'd done our pizzas were delivered by a very puzzled delivery boy. I paid him and tipped him. Elvis thought this was very droll. He told me that when he was at Graceland he often sent his private plane to the Colorado Gold Mine Company in Denver simply because they served great peanut butter and jelly sandwiches on Italian loaves. He could, of course, have had a chef make up the sandwiches. But sending a plane to Denver just to buy a sandwich appealed to his sense of the absurd. Just as sitting in a café and ordering a take away amused him. Sadly, the pizzas were leathery and inedible. We abandoned them.

By now it was very dark and very cold. We found a café near to our apartment in the Rue Du Dr Finlay and ordered glasses of vin chaud while we studied the menu. When I looked up to see if Elvis had decided what he wanted to eat I noticed that his attention seemed to be elsewhere. I followed his gaze and saw that he was looking at one of the waitresses who was sitting at a table in a far corner wrapping cutlery inside paper napkins in the way that cafés sometimes do. She looked to be in her late teens or early twenties. She seemed to be concentrating on what she was doing but every now and then she would look across in Elvis's direction and peep at him under lowered eyelids. She looked like a nice girl.

`Wander over and tell her I'd like to see her later,' murmured Elvis. `Get her name and find out what time she finishes here.'

I stared at him. `I can't do that!'

`Of course you can,' insisted Elvis. He looked at me and frowned. He seemed genuinely puzzled. `Why can't you?'

`Because you're not Elvis Presley anymore,' I whispered. `That's not the way normal guys pick up girls.'

`She'll meet me,' said Elvis. `They always do.'

`They always did,' I told him. `But you were Elvis then.'

`I'm still the same person.'

'No, you're not. You're a good looking, well dressed guy in his early forties. And she seems interested in you. But you're no longer the world's greatest rock star. You can't just snap your fingers and expect her to undress, lie down and wait for the earth to move. You have to woo her first.'

Elvis stared at me. 'Woo her? What does woo her mean?'

'Charm her. Ask her about herself. Tell her how beautiful she is. Take her for a drink. Take her to the cinema. Take her dancing.'

Elvis looked me as if I were mad. He was clearly interested in taking her somewhere, but I got the impression he was not planning to go for a drink, see a film or go dancing. He shook his head from side to side as if in quiet despair at my reluctance and failure to understand the way of his world, stood up, turned on the full smile and walked over to where the girl was working. Three minutes later he was back.

'What's the time?'

I looked at my watch. 'Twenty to nine.'

'When we've finished eating, you can leave me here.'

Now it was my turn to look puzzled. I added another sachet of sugar to my vin chaud and stirred the steaming wine with my spoon.

'She finishes at ten. When we've finished eating I'll have another of these and I'll wait for her here.' He lifted his glass of hot wine as he spoke.

'Where are you taking her?'

Elvis looked at me. 'To the flat, of course.'

I looked at him. 'Don't take out your contact lenses and for God's sake don't start singing.'

I ate a cheese omelette, fries and a delicious side dish which the French call crudités and which consists of finely grated carrots, tomatoes, beetroot and celeriac on a plate with chopped hard-boiled egg. Elvis ate a hamburger, without a bun but with French fries. I wondered what the Graceland crowd would have said if they'd seen him sitting eating a plain hamburger and fries. In the bad old days he'd have had the burger smothered with cheese and onions. And he'd have eaten it two or three times at a single sitting. Elvis still enjoyed bacon, eggs, burgers, peanut jelly and all the other not-terribly-good-for-you foods which he'd always loved but now he ate them in moderation. He used to eat enough to feed a Las Vegas audience; now he ate only enough to feed a man with a waistline to protect. He had, however, retained his sweet tooth and when he'd finished the burger he ordered, ate and obviously enjoyed two thirds of a banana split. That was another difference. In the Graceland days he would never leave anything on his plate. I left Elvis to order himself another vin chaud and to pay the bill. I picked up our shopping bags, headed back to the apartment, which was no more than a ten minute stroll away from the café, and spent the rest of the evening lying on my bed reading the newspapers we'd bought.

I looked at the clock when I heard Elvis come in. It was twenty past ten. The giggling and squealing started about two minutes after that. I would, I decided, have to buy myself a tape player with a set of headphones.

It was clear that even when Elvis wasn't Elvis his idea of wooing wasn't quite the same as everyone else's.

Chapter Twenty Six

The waitress stayed for breakfast. Her name was Dominique, she was 19-years-old and it turned out that when she wasn't wrapping cutlery inside napkins she was an aspiring actress, studying drama at the Jacques Lecoq drama school on the rue due Faubourg St Denis.

I'd woken fairly early, washed, shaved, dressed and joined the queue outside our best local bakery at just after eight.

There were four bakers within a quarter of a mile radius of our flat but it wasn't difficult to spot the one which sold the best baguettes and croissants. Three of the bakers had no queues at all. You could walk in, choose what you wanted and leave within two minutes. The fourth always had a long queue and even with four assistants serving, wrapping and giving change it took customers fifteen minutes to make a purchase. But the wait was worth it.

The locals bought their bread from this bakery because although all four bakeries made their bread on the premises the successful bakery was the only one which always sold produce which was still warm from the ovens. The steady stream of customers made it easier for them to do this, of course. The popular bakery was selling ten times as much bread; the baker had to work flat out to keep up with demand and the stuff on display in the shop never had chance to get cold. On the face of it the other three bakers didn't stand a chance and would never be able to break the stranglehold

But the unsuccessful bakers knew that in France logic invariably takes a back seat to emotion and they struggled on knowing that one day the queue would move and it would, perhaps, be their turn to take their chance; to make vast profits for a while.

The same thing happens in Paris with cafés and restaurants. A café which has been open for years and which has never been particularly popular will suddenly find itself fashionable. There is, perhaps, a dish on the menu which proves attractive or, a waiter or waitress who attracts attention. There may be a good review in one of the Paris newspapers. Or, more likely, a celebrity of some kind decides to eat there; an actor, a musician, a writer, a film director or a politician. And for a while the café will be the only place in Paris to eat and to be seen. People who would have never dreamt of eating there will wait weeks for a reservation. Even when it is freezing cold and pouring with rain there will be queues outside. No one will want to eat in the other half a dozen cafés in the same street. Their waiters will stand around in the doorway smoking and waiting. Their owners will sit in the kitchen waiting for something to cook. The owners' wives will sit behind the tills waiting for a reason to break open the cash float.

But the lucky owner must take full advantage of his good fortune. He must put aside profits from the fat years to help him survive the lean years which will come his way.

For no reason that anyone can put a finger on, the fashionable café will suddenly go out of favour. The reservations will dry up. Overnight, the queues will disappear. The celebrities won't want to be seen there. The waiters will stand in the door way smoking and waiting.

And thus it is with bakeries. One day there is a queue. For months, or maybe even years, a bakery will sell every baguette, every croissant and every pain au raisins that it can produce. The owner will grow fat and complacent. The staff behind the counter will treat the customers with a unique Parisian variety of contempt. The owner will put up his prices, buy a limousine and a cottage by the sea, take a mistress and contemplate retirement to the country.

And then, as though they are suddenly taking revenge for all the queuing, all the over-charging and all the abuse, the customers will move their allegiance to one of the other local bakeries.

I arrived back at the flat at 8.30 am, surrounded by the warm, sweet smell of fresh bread, carrying two country style sesame seed coated baguettes, a country loaf suitable for cutting into slices and a bag of croissants. It is always difficult to resist the yearning to pull the end off a warm baguette, or a piece off a croissant, but I was strong willed and held off temptation.

Elvis was still in bed but Dominique was in the kitchen grinding coffee beans. Her hair was wet and she was wearing the shirt he'd been wearing the day before. She had his tie wrapped around her waist as a belt. It suddenly occurred to me, quite inconsequentially, that we needed to go and buy some new clothes. We had only two or three shirts and one pair of shoes apiece.

The shirt was much too big for her and it reached down to her knees. The tie did give it a little shape. Her feet were bare and her toe nails were painted crimson. We said good morning to each other and exchanged names. I put the bread down on the kitchen table. I desperately hoped that Elvis would get up soon. I really didn't want to have a conversation with Dominique until I knew what he had told her. Had he told her that we were businessmen working in Paris? If so, what sort of business were we in? Were we holidaymakers? Had he remembered that we were both English? Or, after three months of enforced celibacy, had he been too excited to waste time on conversation? I didn't really care what he'd told her as long as it wasn't the truth. And, from looking at her face, I knew he hadn't told her the truth.

Just then I heard Elvis singing `Love Me Tender' in the shower.

Chapter Twenty Seven

'I'd better just check that there are some towels in the bathroom,' I said, talking as loudly as I could without sounding like a complete idiot.

'Oh, there are two fresh towels left,' said Dominique. Her English was excellent. 'I used only the one towel.' She smiled. 'A blue one. The smallest because I am not so very big.'

'I'll check the soap and shampoo,' I said.

'Oh there is plenty of both,' Dominique assured me. 'I used only a tiny little bit of shampoo.'

Elvis was in full voice. I was now beginning to worry about the neighbours hearing him.

'He gets a rash if he doesn't use a special shampoo,' I lied. 'He forgets sometime. I'll just make sure…'

'OK,' she said, smiling. I wondered what she was thinking. She probably thought I wanted to talk to Elvis about her. To ask how long she was staying, perhaps. Or maybe she thought I was gay and jealous. I didn't care. I had to tell Elvis to stop singing. 'Shall I make the coffee?' she asked.

'Yes, please! There are cups in one of the cupboards.' I started to say which one and then realised I couldn't remember where they were.

'I will find them,' said Dominique. 'Don't worry. But you must both hurry up while the croissants are still warm.'

Five minutes later the three of us were sitting around the kitchen table drinking excellent coffee and eating fresh croissants. Because he had no clean shirts and no dressing gown Elvis just had one towel wrapped around his waist and another draped over his shoulders. I realised that we would have to find two new apartments, not one. I didn't want to spend the rest of my life watching Elvis canoodling over breakfast.

'Did you remember to use your special shampoo?' Dominique asked Elvis.

He looked at her and frowned.

'For your allergy,' I said.

He looked at me, still frowning.

'He sometimes forgets,' I explained to Dominique.

'I've got a terrible memory,' said Elvis. 'Especially when I haven't had enough sleep.'

'You should have stayed in bed,' she said. 'I have to be in class this morning. But you could have slept a little more. Older men need more rest.'

I had a mouthful of coffee and I nearly choked on it.

'Why did you stop singing?' Dominique asked Elvis. 'You have a very good voice.'

'Oh, the acoustics in there are perfect,' I said. 'Everyone sounds good when they sing in the shower room. He sounds like Sinatra.'

'I don't think so,' said Dominique. 'Not Sinatra. More like one of those old rockers. Like Johnny Hallyday.'

I laughed as though this were funny. Elvis tried to laugh but it didn't sound much like a laugh to me. 'What time does your class finish?' Elvis asked her.

'My morning class finishes at twelve. Then I have a class at two. And then I must go to the café until ten. I work very hard.'

'Do you finish at ten again?'

'Yes. But I cannot see you afterwards. My boyfriend is back tonight.'

This time it was Elvis who nearly choked.

Dominique stroked his hair, as a woman might stroke a cat's fur, or a mother stroke a daughter's hair. 'My boyfriend is a very jealous man,' she said. 'I must be there for him. He plays in a band and has a very great talent. One day he will be famous.' She paused for a moment. 'He loves me very much though I suspect that last night he probably slept with one of the groupies.' She stopped stroking it and looked carefully at Elvis's hair. 'You are wise to have your hair cut short,' she said after a moment. 'You have a small naked patch here. I believe it will soon be much bigger.' She looked at the clock, stood up and unfastened the tie around her waist. She had not fastened any of the buttons and the shirt fell open. She either didn't notice or, more likely, simply didn't care. 'I must go,' she said to Elvis. 'Thank you for the loving.'

Elvis, who had gone bright red, murmured something I didn't catch.

'You should not be ashamed of your singing,' she told him as she slipped out of the shirt. She left it where it fell and didn't bother to pick it up. She didn't seem to notice that she was now completely naked. 'You have a good voice. You should sing more when you take a shower.' She wagged a finger at me. 'You should not stop him singing,' she said. 'He is not at all a bad singer.'

I closed my eyes and prayed that Elvis wouldn't say a word.

'If he had done more singing when he was a younger man and if he had been properly trained at a school…who knows?' She smiled as she delivered this patronising coup de grace and then disappeared into the bedroom.

Three minutes later she was dressed in the clothes she had been wearing when we'd seen her in the café. She kissed Elvis on the lips and kissed me three times on my cheeks. And then she was gone.

I looked at Elvis. He did not look well and for a moment I was worried that he might explode or burst into flames. He looked at me. Neither of us spoke.

Elvis and I finished the coffee and the croissants without much in the way of conversation. I knew him well enough to know that there was no point in trying to talk about his short-lived romance. I don't think he'd expected it to be a one night stand. Or, if he had, he had not anticipated that Dominique would have the same expectations.

'We ought to go and buy some clothes,' I told him. 'I haven't got a clean shirt and I've run out of clean socks and pants. You must be the same.'

'Yep,' said Elvis.

'If we buy some washing powder while we're out then when we get back we could try to make the washing machine work.'

'Yep.'

I cleared away the breakfast crocks and cleaned out the coffee bean grinder and the coffee machine.

'You'll need to put a shirt on,' I told Elvis. I was beginning to sound, and feel, like a mother hen.

He looked down, nodded, stood up and disappeared into his bedroom. Two minutes later he came out wearing a rumpled, dirty shirt that he had worn when we'd travelled on the plane from Ireland.

We put on our overcoats, went down to the street and did some basic shopping. We found everything we needed within half a mile of our apartment and stocked up with bags full of shirts, socks and other items. We then visited the mayor's office and started the administrative process that would end in our obtaining our cartes de sejour – the permits that British passport holders needed then in order to live and work in France. This promised to be the exactly the sort of nightmare I had expected it to be. I was not in the slightest bit surprised when we were told that we had to produce our passports, a fistful of photographs of ourselves and a collection of utility bills. I was surprised they didn't want our hat sizes. Bureaucrats everywhere collect these bits and pieces of useless nonsense in order to fill their filing cabinets and give themselves a sense of importance. In France, the whole thing can take weeks or even months. And if there is a strike or a go slow or an essential member of staff is away ill or on holiday the process can probably extend over several lifetimes. French bureaucrats are the most assiduous in the world and, like all their countrymen, are addicted to saying 'No'. A friend of mine insists that the first word of French that a baby learns is 'Non' and that the first complete sentence it masters is 'It is not possible'.

Knowing this, I said to the bureaucrat in charge: 'I am sure it will not be possible to do this quickly.'

He lowered his head and looked at me over the top of his spectacles.

I repeated my challenge.

He frowned. All French citizens are born contrary; they love to argue and prove everyone else wrong. They particularly enjoy making foreigners look stupid. 'It may be impossible in other offices,' he said, 'but here we can do these things very quickly. You may pick up your cards in two hours.' A woman at a desk behind him, who had overheard his boast, looked up and stared at him in absolute horror.

We shook hands, left and when we got outside we stopped at a café we hadn't visited before and ordered two glasses of vin chaud. We sat at a pavement table which was warmed by a huge outdoor gas heater. The sky was black and it was clearly going to rain soon. The waitress looked to be about 105 years old. Judging by the way she walked she seemed to have bad knees and bad feet and judging by the way she worked she had a pretty bad memory. We had to tell her twice what we wanted to drink.

'Maybe I'd be safer off pulling this one,' said Elvis.

I looked at him.

'That other one had quite a mouth on her.'

I grinned. 'Really?'

Elvis grinned back and shrugged.

We sipped our drinks. As expected it started to rain. Passers-by hurried along the pavement. The ones carrying umbrellas stopped under the shelter of the café awning and struggled to open them.

'I need to get a job,' I told Elvis.

He looked at me as if I'd just told him I was going to become an astronaut, or set off to go round the world on roller skates.

'I can't live off your money,' I explained.

'Why not?' He seemed genuinely puzzled.

'Because I can't! I'm not going to leech on you.'

Elvis looked surprised. He had, after all, become accustomed to being surrounded by people who lived off him. At Graceland there had been a small army of relatives and friends who'd been hired to do things for him, to look after him, to entertain him, to play with him and to comfort him when he was feeling low. He had taken it for granted that he would provide for them and their families and, probably, their families' families. 'What am I going to do all day if you're at work?'

'Explore Paris, sit in cafés, read books and meet girls.'

'I thought we'd do those things together,' said Elvis.

And I suddenly realised that he was afraid of being alone. He hadn't been by himself for years. With a shock I knew that without companions he would be unable to survive. I think that deep down I had known this for some time. I'd certainly suspected it. But knowing that it was true was still a shock.

'I can't just live off you,' I told him. 'I can't. I would feel like…'

'Like a whore?'

'Yes, I guess so.'

Elvis nodded. He sipped at his vin chaud. 'I do like this drink,' he said. 'Never had it before you introduced me to it.'

'Keeps the chill out.' It had started to rain heavily now but we were dry and surprisingly warm.

'Yep.'

We sat and watched the passers-by for a while. It is difficult not to feel superior when you're sitting in the warm, sipping an intoxicating drink, while other people are rushing by in the rain. I confess I do always feel a little guilty about it but there is no denying that it is a very pleasant feeling.

Across the street a few musicians started to collect underneath a stone archway. As each newcomer arrived he put down his instrument case and shook hands and exchanged cheek kisses with everyone who was already there. Since each person kissed everyone else three times this took a great deal of time. The Parisians don't do the sort of mwah mwah, make-up preserving kisses that are popular in other countries. The Parisians insist on three full blooded kisses, using two sets of lips and four cheeks. In between kissing and shaking hands they took out their instruments. There were four saxophones, three trumpets, a French horn, a tuba and something I couldn't identify. There was even a man with a small drum kit. Two or three of the musicians had brought music stands which they set up in front of them. As this process was being completed three girls arrived and took off their coats. They were wearing tight fitting dresses but carried no instruments. They were clearly either going to sing or to dance. I hoped they were going to dance because if they just stood there and sang they would probably freeze to death.

I remembered from my previous life in the city that pick-up bands are enormously popular and common in Paris and can be regularly found in the parks and squares. They can most commonly be found playing where tourists are to be found in the greatest profusion; near the fountain in the Place St Michel, on the steps below Sacre Coeur, in the Tuileries Gardens, in the Champs de Mars and in the Place des Vosges, but quite a few of them simply set up near a café or on a wide stretch of pavement. Some are professionals, some are music students, others are simply enthusiastic amateurs.

'So what are we going to do then?'

I looked at him.

'If you're going to get a job then I want a job too.'

I picked up my vin chaud and took a sip. I hadn't expected this.

'You don't have to get a job. There are quite a few dollars left from the bagful Vernon gave us and once we've turned the diamonds into cash you'll have enough money for the rest of your life.'

There was a long silence. The old waitress came to our table, told us that she was going off duty and asked us to pay. I paid her and gave her a decent tip. She screwed up the paper slip which had come with the drinks and left it on the table to show the waiter replacing her that we had paid.

'I don't think I can just be by myself all day,' said Elvis quietly. 'I've always been with people. I'd get lonely and depressed if there was no one around to talk to.'

The small band across the street started warming up; each musician playing a few notes to satisfy himself that he still knew what to do, and that his instrument hadn't turned into a food mixer or a toaster while he hadn't been looking.

'There are a lot of tour companies in Paris,' I said. 'We could try to get jobs as couriers – showing people round the city, making sure they don't get lost crossing the pavement from the coach into their hotel.'

'Don't you need lots of training for that?'

'I shouldn't think so. Just a large brightly coloured umbrella. Preferably something that looks unusual. You tie a scarf or a few ribbons to it.'

'In case it rains?'

'No, no. When you take a group of tourists round one of the sights you have to hold up an umbrella so that they've got something to follow. Like the children of Hamlin following the pied piper.'

'But why do you need to tie a scarf to the umbrella?'

'A friend of mine once had a job as a courier and he lost an entire group of 34 tourists. They were from Burnley.'

'Where's Burnley?'

'Oh, somewhere in the North of England. It doesn't matter. My pal had an ordinary black umbrella which he held up in the air so that his party could follow him. Unfortunately, a group of students from the Sorbonne had just finished their exams and were wandering around looking for ways to cause mischief. One of the students acquired an identical black umbrella, held it up and 'kidnapped' my pal's entire group. They followed the wrong umbrella for miles and miles. It took my pal four hours, and a visit to the police station, to find them. They'd been taken to the Pere Lachaise cemetery and abandoned there; they were cold, hungry, exhausted and very, very angry.'

'I don't think I know enough about Paris to be a guide,' said Elvis.

'You don't really need to know much,' I said. I noticed that the rain had stopped and the pedestrians passing by had put down their umbrellas. 'As long as you know that the one which looks as if it hasn't been finished is the Eiffel Tower and the church which had a hunchback crawling across the roof is Notre Dame.'

'What hunchback?' asked Elvis.

'We can think of something else to do,' I said. I suddenly felt an inexplicable pang of pity for poor old Victor Hugo. The cathedral of Notre Dame, which had been badly damaged during the French Revolution because it contained statues which were thought to represent French kings, had been in decline until his novel 'The Hunchback of Notre Dame' was published. It was Hugo himself who organised a petition which led to the restoration of the cathedral in the 1820's. I love the place. The fact that it is situated on an island in the middle of the River Seine means that it is probably the most romantically positioned ecclesiastical building anywhere in the world, and the gothic design means that it looks as good in the mist and dull half-light of a winter afternoon as it does in the bright sunshine of a summer morning.

What hunchback indeed.

The band across the street started playing a piece of jazz which I didn't recognise. The three women who had taken off their coats started singing and dancing. The archway in which they were dancing, and in which the musicians were playing, wasn't very wide but miraculously they all managed to keep out of one another's way.

'They're pretty good at not falling over one another,' I said.

'They're used to playing in small clubs,' said Elvis. 'When I started out we did open air gigs where they didn't have stages. We played on the back of a lorry. It wasn't a very big lorry. I couldn't move around much without falling off the darned thing so I just moved my hips from side to side.'

I looked at him to see if he was joking.

'Honest!'

'I never knew that!'

'I never told anyone.'

The band had finished its first number and had moved straight onto the second. It was too cold for them to stand around chatting. I could see a beautiful rainbow arching through the sky. When insurance companies, and others with no sense of joy and wonderment, describe Acts of God they are always talking about hurricanes and earthquakes. I prefer to think of rainbows and sunsets as Acts of God.

I drank the last of my vin chaud. Elvis had already finished his.

'Do you want another?'

Elvis thought for a moment. 'No, I don't think I do. I'll pick up a cake on the way home.'

I laughed at the non sequitur. Elvis had already discovered that most of the bakeries which can be found every few hundred yards in Paris don't just sell bread and croissants. The majority also sell cakes, pastries, tarts and exotic creations built out of meringue, cream and chocolate.

We picked up our shopping bags and returned to the Mayor's office. The bureaucrat who had accepted my challenge looked at me arrogantly. 'You see,' he said, holding up our residence permits, 'nothing is impossible in this office!' We accepted our cards, thanked and congratulated him, shook hands all round and left before anyone decided that we all knew one another well enough to start exchanging cheek kisses.

Outside, back in the real world, we took our lives into our hands and crossed the road. This is always a hazardous business in Paris. French motorists regard pedestrians as fair game and if you want to avoid becoming a hood ornament on a battered Renault you must take great care when crossing even the narrowest, least impressive of roads. Some of the wider avenues require courage, timing and considerable levels of athleticism to get from one side to the other in good health. Timing is everything and you must, of course, always keep a hand free so that you can make rude gestures. A few of the larger areas require more courage than would be required to swim through a mile of shark infested sea. Very few people are, for example, brave enough to try to cross the Place de la Concorde on foot.

Once we'd safely negotiated the speeding traffic we both paused to toss notes into the black felt fedora one of the musicians had placed upside down on the ground, and headed back towards our temporary residence.

'They're good,' said Elvis.

On the way back to our flat, we stopped at a bakery and bought one cake each. Elvis chose a small tart filled with strawberries and topped with fresh cream. I selected a cricket ball sized confection made out of meringue, filled with cream and covered in chocolate. The Parisian name for this delight was, at the time, a tete de negre, though political correctness ensures that these exceptionally scrumptious but admittedly sickly delights are now known rather prosaically as meringues au chocolat.

And from a newspaper kiosk I picked up a locally published English language newspaper which, I rather hoped, might contain some job opportunities. Life might have been easier if we'd just bought the cakes and not bothered with the newspaper.

Chapter Twenty Eight

We ate out that evening at one of the local cafés. There were so many cafés in the locality that it wasn't difficult to avoid the establishment where Dominique worked.

   Elvis ordered a steak and a salad. My stomach was still struggling to digest the tete de negre I'd greedily and rather foolishly consumed, so I contented myself with a popular French café dish called a croque monsieur. This is a grilled ham and cheese sandwich which is usually made with emmenthal or gruyere cheese and served with béchamel sauce. French cafés have been serving this quick dish since before the First World War. There's a variation known as croquet-madame which is served with a fried or poached egg perched on the top. We shared a bottle of the house red wine. In Paris the house wines are usually somewhat better than much more expensive wines served in British or American restaurants.

   I heard a commotion and looked around. A man of about 30 had stood up and was putting on his coat. In standing up he had knocked over his chair. He wore a thin moustache, sharp sideburns and a silk suit. His companion, a woman about five years younger, took off a ring and handed it to him. He looked at it as if checking to make sure that he wasn't being palmed off with a cheap substitute, and then put the ring into his breast pocket. The woman, who was wearing a white blouse and a dark skirt and had a black coat folded over the chair next to her, folded her arms. She was dark haired and petite but she still managed to look furious and rather ferocious. When her companion had stalked out the woman unfolded her arms, picked up her glass and drained it. She then called the waiter and ordered a replacement.

   As we ate I looked through the 'situations vacant' page in the newspaper I'd bought. An American woman wanted someone to walk her two dogs. A small vegetarian restaurant in the 10th arrondissement wanted someone to do the washing up. A tour company wanted someone to stand on the Champs Élysées and hand out promotional leaflets. A restaurant chain wanted actors and actresses to dress up as animals and parade up and down outside their stores to promote their new range of family meals. Even the advertisers wanting to fill these rather menial posts wanted references and details of previous experience. It wouldn't have surprised me if they'd wanted qualifications too, though I wasn't quite sure precisely what sort of qualifications might be regarded as appropriate for dish washers or dog walkers.

After a while I gave up reading the job adverts and flicked through the rest of the paper. As a former journalist I couldn't help noticing that most of the articles were badly written and at least half of the photographs were out of focus. The newspaper was, in short, rather a mess.

`Anything promising?' asked Elvis, who had finished his steak.

I shook my head. `Nothing. Unless you want to dress up as a teddy bear. Do you want coffee?'

We ordered two coffees, and sat in silence for a while. There is always something to watch if you pick a table in the window. I love watching Parisians park their cars. In most other countries, if a driver is sitting in a car which is fifteen feet long and he finds a parking space which is fourteen feet long he will curse and then drive on. This isn't the French way. In Paris the driver makes the space fit his car, rather than the other way round. He will simply reverse into the space as hard as he can and bump the car behind back as far as it will go. This inevitably means that the car into which he has backed will be shunted into the car behind it. And so on and on. The driver will then nudge the car at the front of the space he wants to drive into. And eventually he will get his fifteen foot long car into the fourteen foot space because he will have turned it into a fifteen and a half foot long space. The fun is, of course, repeated when a driver of one of the cars which has been shunted, and which is now bumper to bumper with the adjacent vehicles, wants to move his car. In most countries a driver who found that he was sandwiched by two cars whose bumpers touched his own would probably jump up and down and start tearing out hair. In Paris, the driver simply climbs into his car and bumps the cars either side of him until there is enough space available for him to drive out into the traffic. This may sometimes involve a good deal of engine revving because a dozen cars or more may have to be moved along. When the driver can zoom out into the traffic he does so without signalling, of course, because signalling is sissy and not something Parisian drivers do unless they intend to drive in a dead straight line and want to confuse the motorist travelling behind them. I once asked a Frenchman why drivers in Paris never give any signals. 'We French are a very private peoples,' he said. 'It is no one else's business where we are going.'

I wondered if perhaps I should get in touch with one or two of the English newspapers I knew to see if they needed a Paris correspondent. And then I quickly realised that I couldn't do that. There was far too big a chance that someone would recognise me.

'Back in a minute,' I said to Elvis. I headed for the stairs down to the toilettes. French cafés often have their toilets in the basement. If there is a staircase visible in a café it's a pretty good bet that the route to the loos will be down the stairs.

I was away for no more than three or four minutes at the most but when I returned to our table Elvis was missing. I looked around and saw him sitting at a table on the other side of the café. He was sitting next to the woman whose companion had stormed out just a few minutes earlier. Elvis was smiling. She was laughing and appeared to have forgotten her worries. She was a few years older than the sort of girl Elvis usually liked but if there had been no other woman available Elvis would have probably hit on a 60-year-old cleaning woman with her hair wrapped in a headscarf.

I paid our bill, pushed the terrible newspaper into my coat pocket, and headed for the doors at the front of the café. I made sure my route between the tables took me past Elvis.

'Are you staying?' I asked.

'For a while,' said Elvis. He winked.

I went back to our apartment, had a shower and went to bed with a copy of 'John McNab', a novel by John Buchan which I'd bought from a second hand bookstall by the river Seine.

I couldn't help feeling that our lives were beginning to fall into a pattern.

Chapter Twenty Nine

When I awoke the following morning Elvis wasn't in the flat. There was no sign of him and his bed hadn't been slept in. I walked to the bakery, bought a baguette and a bag of croissants, and then made my breakfast. As I ate I re-read the local newspaper I'd bought. It was printed once a week and called `Americans in Paris' and although it was primarily aimed at Americans it clearly catered for all English speaking expatriates and visitors. There were interviews with artistes passing through Paris, features about Americans who had settled in Paris and small pieces of news that might interest Americans and others who spoke English. A quarter of the newspaper was taken up with classified advertising. There were a few advertisements from students looking for accommodation, adverts from impecunious flat dwellers looking for someone with whom they could share their space and their rent, adverts from people leaving Paris and hoping to sell their belongings rather than try to lug them back across the Atlantic or the Channel, adverts from people trying to sell their services (`I will walk your dog', `French lessons given', `Driver looking for work as chauffeur') and, of course, a couple of columns of lonely hearts adverts.

Finally, and most importantly, there were plenty of job advertisements. I went back to the relevant pages and carried on working my way through them. The trouble was that all the employers advertising decent or even half-decent jobs wanted references, qualifications and experience. And we had no references we could produce, no qualifications we could offer and no experience we could talk about.

But there was one small ray of sunshine. Once I had read the whole paper I knew damned well that I could write much better articles than the journalists currently working on the paper. But what about Elvis? Could he write? From what I knew about him it didn't seem very likely. His talents and skills lay in other directions. And then I suddenly remembered that at Graceland I'd seen Elvis fooling around with cameras and he had, of course, taken my passport photos. I hadn't seen any of the pictures he'd taken but I was confident he could take better photographs than whoever was taking the paper's snaps. A child of six could have taken better pictures. Even then, back in the late 1970's, cameras were fairly simple to use.

I waited for a while, sitting in the kitchen drinking coffee I didn't want and eating a third croissant I should have left in the bag. Then I decided to go out for a walk. I left a note for Elvis and headed down to the river. I sat on a bench for a while and watched the boats going up and down the Seine. Many barge owners live on their boats and you can see children playing and washing hanging out to dry on rope lines. Sometimes there will be a small car parked precariously at the back of the vessel. It's difficult not to envy them their small, safe, private worlds; of the world and yet not quite in it, in it and yet not quite of it. After an hour or so I headed back to the flat. There was still no one there. I ripped up my note and made myself yet another cup of coffee.

Elvis turned up at half past eleven.

`Where have you been?' I heard myself demanding. I felt embarrassed as soon as I had spoken, realising that I sounded like a fussy mother or a jealous wife.

`Sorry,' apologised Elvis. `I should have telephoned.'

I waved aside the apology. `No you shouldn't,' I told him. `It's just that I'm still a bit paranoid. I keep thinking someone will recognise you. Or that you'll start singing when you aren't in the shower.'

`I miss singing,' said Elvis, rather sadly. `Miss it lots.'

`Want a croissant?' I asked.

`No thanks,' he said, smiling. `I ate. Edith made me a crispy bacon sandwich.'

`Edith?'

`Like the singer. That little French one. Apparently her parents were huge fans.'

`You had a good time?'

`Terrific.'

It turned out that Edith, the woman who'd taken Elvis home, worked in a department store as an assistant buyer. The man with whom she'd had a row had been her fiancé. Elvis didn't know his name. They'd had a row because the Frenchman, clearly a traditionalist, had told her that he wanted her to give up working when they got married. It took women in France a long time to obtain the sort of rights enjoyed by women elsewhere. French women only got the vote in 1945 and until 1965 a Frenchman could legally forbid his wife to go to work if he wanted her to stay at home. In her anger Edith had given him back his ring. Elvis, quick thinking and fast acting, had caught her, adroitly and neatly, on the rebound.

'She had an apartment near the Bois de something,' said Elvis.

'Boulogne?'

'That's it. The Bois de Boulogne. Nice little place but it was miles out of the city. I thought we were never going to get there last night. We went on buses. And it took me ages to get a cab back.'

I wondered how long it had been since Elvis had travelled on an ordinary, commercial bus.

'Why didn't you bring her back here?'

Elvis shrugged. 'She wanted to go to her place.'

'Are you seeing her again?'

'Doubt it,' said Elvis. 'Her fiancé came round this morning. He brought back her ring.'

'Oops,' I said, wincing. 'Did he see you?'

Elvis shook his head. 'I stayed in the bedroom. She kept him in the living room.'

'Didn't he notice anything?'

'I don't think so. No, I'm sure he didn't. He seemed very full of himself. Jabber, jabber, jabber. Lots of that French stuff. At least I guess it was probably French. That would be favourite, wouldn't it?'

I said that since we were in Paris it probably would have been French they were speaking.

'I didn't understand anything they said. But I think he must have apologised or, at least, talked her round because they kissed and made up and I could hear a hell of a lot of smoochy stuff going on. When he'd gone she came into the bedroom and told me she'd said she looked tired because she'd been crying all night.'

'A quick thinking woman!'

Elvis nodded. 'She showed me the ring, which looked pretty expensive. Apparently he does something in an advertising agency. And then she took off her dressing gown and came back to bed.' He smiled. 'It was chilly. I don't think she had the heating switched up very high.'

I couldn't help grinning. Elvis's legendary charm seemed to have survived his death.

'What did you do with yourself?' he asked. 'Did you find yourself a lady?'

I shook my head. It occurred to me that if I were going to find a woman I should perhaps ask Elvis for some lessons. I'd never seen anyone pick up women with such consummate ease. On the other hand, I still hadn't quite recovered from my rather unnerving experience in Chicago. If I had found a woman to go to bed with I would have probably spent the night waiting for an angry husband to leap out of the bathroom or in through the bedroom window. 'I had an early night and read a good book,' I confessed. 'But I think I might have found us jobs we might be able to do. Can you use a camera?'

'Of course I can! I used to play around with the cameras when photographers were setting up their shots. We did a lot of photo shoots at the house. And I had some good equipment at Graceland. Pity. Perhaps I should have bought it with me.'

'Right!' I said. 'Put on a clean shirt. We're going to try to fix ourselves a couple of jobs.'

Chapter Thirty

The offices of *The American in Paris* were housed in a building in the Rue Bonaparte a wonderfully old-fashioned street in the sixth arrondissement. (*The American in Paris* is not, of course, the real name of the publication. As far as I'm aware there has never been any publication in Paris with that name.) On the ground floor the neighbouring buildings were largely occupied by art dealers, picture framers and antique specialists. The higher floor contained a few small offices but from the bedding draped out of the windows it seemed that the majority of the buildings were occupied by private residents. In those days the French still hung their bedding out of their windows to give it a good airing. They did this even in freezing cold weather, believing that cold air helped to kill bugs. The building looked as if it had been built three or four hundred years ago and not touched since then. The stonework outside was chipped and at street level a number of bullet holes were visible – mementoes, no doubt, of the various wars that had been fought on the city's streets. Looking up it seemed clear that the building's window frames were all original and most of them were at least a century past their use-by-date. The glass in the windows had that slightly wobbly look that very old glass always has and even the dirt on the glass in the windows looked to be at least three centuries old. The owners and inhabitants of the building clearly had things other than property maintenance on their minds. And why not? The average Parisian will always believe that there are more important things in life than rotten soffits and pitted stonework. It occurred to me that it was a good job that the building was, like just about every other building in Paris, firmly fixed to its neighbours. If one Parisian building ever falls down the rest will collapse like a row of dominoes.

In the lobby on the ground floor, the wall on the left contained a couple of dozen wooden mailboxes. Each one had been labelled, relabelled and relabelled yet again as tenants had arrived, left and been replaced. Several of the mailbox doors were broken and some mail, mostly circulars, had spilt out and was lying on the floor. On the right hand wall there was a list of the building's occupants. The ground floor was taken up by an art gallery, the first, second and third floors seemed to be occupied by residential tenants and the top two floors were home for several businesses. The offices of *The American in Paris* were listed as being right at the very top of the building, on the fifth floor.

There was no lift and to reach the fifth floor we had to climb a narrow, rickety wooden staircase which creaked a good deal as we ascended. There was no carpet and the centre of each tread had been worn down by many thousands of feet. The stone walls and the wooden floors meant that Elvis and I made quite a clatter as we climbed up. As we made our way up the staircase we paused for a few moments to let an old man creep past us, heading downstairs. He had terrible arthritis in both hands and, presumably, in his leg joints and supported himself with two wooden walking sticks, one in each hand. He had a shopping bag with long handles looped over his head. He was smartly dressed, in a sports jacket and flannels, a waistcoat, a neatly pressed shirt, a sober tie and a pair of well-polished brogues and considering the horrifying way that his fingers were swollen and distorted he must have spent ages getting himself ready for his shopping trip. Just tying his tie must have been an ordeal in itself. It took him several minutes to make it down one flight of stairs so heaven knows how long it took him to get down to street level. And I hate to think how long it took him to get back up again. The French, I was learning, do like to be independent. In Britain, a man with such a disability would have expected the State to provide someone to do his shopping for him. I didn't realise it at the time but in France, the average citizen would rather die of starvation or exhaustion than demean himself by asking for help from the State.

When we reached the top floor we looked round but could see no sign of a newspaper office. It was very dark. There were no windows on the landing and the one light bulb, which hung from the ceiling on an old and frayed piece of flex, didn't work. Though the gloom we found that there were two doors. One appeared to lead to an accountant's office and the other to the offices of a theatrical producer and artistes' agent. The doors were scruffy and the notices telling us what lay behind were cracked and faded. Neither of these enterprises looked particularly prosperous. And neither of them appeared to be *The American in Paris*.

I was about to knock on the door of the theatrical producer's offices, to ask if anyone there knew where we could find the newspaper's offices, when Elvis drew my attention to a narrow door that looked as if it led to a cupboard – the sort of modest recess which might be used to store cleaning materials such as brooms and brushes. A small creased postcard had been pinned to the door. Written on it, in pencil, in capitals, was the word 'Private' and below that the words *The American in Paris*.

I opened the door and, behind it, found another staircase. This one was even narrower and steeper than the main staircase. I realised that it led up to accommodation which had originally been designed for use by servants. Rather nervously, we climbed this narrow staircase. I went first. Elvis followed. As we ascended it occurred to me that if I had been any bigger I wouldn't have been able to get up without my hips rubbing against both walls. As it was there was only an inch or so clearance on each side. At the top of this narrow staircase there was a solid looking door. In the middle of the door a piece of paper had pinned upon which had been handwritten the simple warning: 'Mind Your Head'. I opened the door, ducked down to avoid banging my head on the lintel, and almost fell down onto my face because I completely missed the six inch step down into the room beyond. Elvis, following close behind me, managed to avoid falling down the step but hit his head on the lintel.

The first, and only, thing we saw when we had recovered were huge piles of newspapers, all neatly tied up with string. The newspapers, which all seemed to be copies of the latest edition, were stacked, at least five feet high, like a barricade at the top of the staircase. I half expected to see a couple of soldiers poke their heads and rifles over the top. In front of this paper barricade there was just enough room for the two of us to stand.

A small gap between two piles of bound newspapers offered the only way forward. I edged into the gap and through to the other side. There, sitting at a desk and pecking away with two fingers at an old Royal typewriter, was one of the fattest people I've ever seen. He was wearing a white shirt, a bow tie and what looked like the trouser half of a pin striped suit. The trousers were held up by a pair of striped braces. I was astonished to see him there because I couldn't understand how on earth he'd managed to squeeze his way up the stairs. He was smoking a huge cigar and was surrounded by a large cloud of blue smoke. He hadn't bothered to remove the band from around the cigar which looked expensive but smelt like old, wet carpet that a large bladdered dog had repeatedly used as a substitute for a tree. The area of desk on each side of his typewriter was buried under about two feet of paper. There were books, newspapers, press releases, photographic prints and sheets of typescript. Some of the sheets of typescript had been scribbled on in red ink. The wall above the fat man contained a dozen hooks on which hung bulldog clips holding strips of proofs, schedules and plans for future issues of the newspaper.

'Excuse me, sorry to interrupt,' I said, apologetically. 'But we're looking for the editor.'

The fat man finished translating his thought into type on the page in front of him and then turned round to look at us. 'Lintel or step?' he asked.

'Step,' I said.

'Lintel,' said Elvis.

The fat man nodded. 'One or the other. Everyone gets done by one or the other.' He took a gulp of red wine from a large glass, peered at us, looking first at me and then at Elvis. 'Who the devil are you?' He had a curiously round skull that looked like a bowling ball, and a pair of startlingly blue eyes. His hair was light grey, almost white, and grew out of his head in strange tufts; as though it had been glued in place by not terribly artistic infants working under the supervision of a teacher with a more wicked sense of humour than might usually be regarded as acceptable.

When I explained that we were looking for work he laughed. It was a surprisingly high pitched laugh, more of a giggle than the rumble I might have expected from a man of his size. 'Are you volunteers?'

'Not exactly,' I said. 'We were hoping you could employ us. I'm a writer and my friend is a photographer.' I told him my name and Elvis told him his.

'You're American?' he asked, looking at Elvis.

'No, sir, I'm English,' drawled Elvis. Some days he could pass for English but at that moment he sounded as American as apple pie, ten gallon hats and boot lace ties.

'He spent a lot of time living in America,' I added. I still hadn't managed to persuade Elvis to stop saying 'Sir' when talking to men who were older than him. It was, I suppose, ingrained in his soul. I had realised that Elvis was, like most people, a mass of contradictions and, deep down, underneath the rock'n'roll lifestyle, lay the heart and spirit of a Mississippi gentleman.

'I was trying to get into show business,' explained Elvis. 'But at heart I'm a photographer. Born with a camera in my hand.'

'Are you American?' I asked the fat man. It was impossible to tell from his accent where he'd originally come from.

'Pretty much,' he replied, enigmatically. 'My name is Carpenter. Hildebrand Carpenter. Everyone calls me Hildy. You're both living in Paris?'

'Yes. We've just moved here.'

'Living together?'

'For the time being?'

'Homosexuals?' He picked up his wine glass and took another gulp. It was a large glass which probably held a third of a litre.

'No, sir!' said Elvis, with possibly rather too much emphasis to be entirely convincing.

'No,' I added.

'Just asking,' said the fat man with a slight shrug. 'I don't care if you fuck elephants.'

I thought that this seemed generous of him, though probably an unlikely and impractical possibility and one fraught with difficulties and both natural and unnatural hazards.

'We're both hetero,' said Elvis firmly. There was a fire in his voice I hadn't heard before and then I remembered that he didn't like homosexuals or homosexuality. I remembered one of the guys at Graceland telling me that while making 'Fun in Acapulco' there was a scene in which Elvis, wearing swimming trunks, was carried up some steps by a bunch of young men. Elvis claimed that one of the actors carrying him tried to hold his penis and was furious about it. He wanted him fired but I don't think anyone on the film set had been able to identify the actor responsible. At Graceland, and in hotels when on tour, the young Elvis was so staunchly heterosexual that he was renowned for taking three or four girls to bed with him at a time, though quite what he managed to do with them all was something of a mystery.

The fat man looked at him, as though unconvinced, and shrugged. 'I need someone to help with the distribution,' he said. 'I can't get up and down the stairs. I had a French kid helping me but he's run off to Alvoriaz to work as a ski bum.'

'What about someone to help writing stories and taking pictures?'

'Maybe, maybe,' agreed the fat man grudgingly. 'Do you know anything about newspapers?' He emptied the wine glass and looked at it rather sadly.

'A little,' I replied, cautiously.

'*The American in Paris* isn't like most other papers,' he said. 'We're fighting the American and British dailies and the French local papers. We have a small, base readership of locals but we sell most of our papers to visitors, tourists, businessmen passing through. We have to make them feel that they're buying an insight into the real Paris – the secret heart and private soul of a city they'd never normally see without living here.'

'Are you the editor?' I asked him, though he obviously was. I really wanted to know who owned the paper.

'Editor, founder, publisher, owner, sub editor, advertising manager and distributor.' He had a curious way of talking, raising his voice a little at the end of every sentence, which meant that everything he said sounded like a question.

'Impressive,' I said. 'That lot would fill up a visiting card very nicely.'

'Can't afford fripperies like visiting cards,' said the fat man. He sounded rather bitter. 'Can't afford salaries either.' A large mackerel tabby cat which had been sleeping on top of one of the piles of newspapers stretched and jumped down to the floor. It then walked slowly over to the fat man and climbed onto his lap.

'Oh,' I said. 'That's a pity. We both need work that pays.' I turned and started to head back towards the top of the stairs. Every publisher I've ever known has always pleaded poverty but I've known very few who didn't make money.

'I'll pay you 25 cents in the franc on every advert you bring me,' said the fat man. I turned round and looked at him. He was stroking the cat and if the cat had been white he would have looked like a baddie in one of the early James Bond movies. The eyes seemed to become bluer and lighter the more I looked at them. He really was very fat. It seemed clear to me that he could not possibly climb up or down the narrow staircase which led to his offices though it wasn't until a week or two later that we found out that he had a small bedroom, bathroom and kitchen on the same floor and was, indeed, a prisoner on the top floor. A boy from the local grocery store delivered his food and other shopping. And for two weeks the delivery boy had been also struggling up and down the stairs with piles of newspapers. 'And the same on every extra copy you manage to sell to a new outlet,' the fat man continued. 'I've always done pretty well with tobacconists, newsagents, bookshops and hotels and cafés catering for tourists. They keep 25% of the cover price and we pick up the copies they don't sell.'

'They don't pay anything unless they've sold some newspapers?'

'Sadly, that is true. Sale or return.' With great gentleness he took the cat from his lap and put it on his desk. He then leant to his left and took a fresh bottle of wine from a wooden crate. He took a Swiss army penknife from his trouser pocket, opened the corkscrew attachment and removed the cork. It was all done very slickly and it was obviously a procedure he had performed many times. He then poured some of the wine into his glass and put the bottle in front of him. He didn't offer either of us a drink.

I nodded. Selling newspapers, magazines and books on a sale or return basis is pretty standard. The publisher always takes all the risks. I noticed that there were at least a dozen empty wine bottles in a box underneath his desk. I wondered how long it had taken him to empty them.

'What happens to the copies they haven't sold?'

'We collect them when we deliver the following weeks papers. We then take them to a fellow who has a couple of market stalls selling fish. He uses the old papers as fish wrappers. He gives me a nice piece of cod and sometimes a crab. And I don't have to pay the city to take away my refuse.' He picked up the cat from the desk and put it back on his lap.

'Why don't you just let the shops throw away the unsold ones?' asked Elvis. 'That would save you the trouble picking them up and taking them to the fish guy.'

'Because they'd lie and say they'd thrown all of them away,' said the fat man, wearily.

'And what will you pay for articles and photographs?' I asked him. 'That's really what we do.'

'Bring me something good and I'll think about it. I'm always looking for exclusive stories. We can't beat the big papers with the ordinary news so we have to find something special.'

Suddenly, a telephone started to ring. The fat man burrowed amongst the papers piled high on his desk, found a black, old-fashioned Bakelite telephone and picked up the handset. He spoke in French for about two minutes and then put the handset back on the receiver. He spoke so quickly and quietly that I couldn't hear what he said. And I couldn't hear any of the conversation at the other end of the line.

'Do you have a car? he asked. He seemed very pleased about something.

'No.'

'Licence?'

I was about to say 'yes' when I suddenly realised that although I'd had a driving licence under my real name I didn't have a licence under my new name. And nor did Elvis. In order to obtain licences we would have to take driving tests. And since I didn't fancy doing that in France we'd probably have to go to England. 'No,' I admitted.

'I can drive,' said Elvis.

I looked at him and frowned. He clearly didn't understand that although Elvis Presley had had a driving licence his new persona did not have one.

'Fine,' said the fat man. 'My main distributor wants another 300 copies of the paper. We seem to be having a good week.' He scribbled an address on the back of a press release promoting a new film and handed it to me. Then he took a set of keys out of his trouser pocket and handed those to Elvis. 'You'll need the van. It's a little grey Citroen and it's parked in the courtyard. It probably needs petrol and I think it could probably do with some oil as well. And maybe a couple of pints of water. There's a garage in the Boulevard St Germain. When you've made the delivery just bring the van back and park it where you found it, if the space is still there. If some French bastard has taken the space just park behind them and block them in. It'll teach them a lesson.''

'What's the paper's circulation?' I asked.

'If an advertiser asks tell them it's just over 10,000 copies a week. They won't believe more than that. But they'll believe 10,000.'

'What's the print run?'

He looked at me, trying to decide how much of the truth to tell me. 'I print 4,000,' he said at last. The lie, the huge difference between his claimed circulation and his print run didn't seem to bother him at all. He waved at the newsprint barricades at the top of the stairs. 'This is what we've got left.'

There were, I guessed, between fifteen hundred and two thousand copies in the stacks. It wasn't difficult to work out that if the fat man was telling the truth about his print run he wasn't making a fortune out of his newspaper.

'Do you have any money?' he asked.

'Not much,' I said cautiously.

'Do you want to invest?'

'What in?'

'In *The American in Paris* of course. 'I'll sell you a quarter share each. You'd both become newspaper proprietors.'

I looked at Elvis who shrugged and made it clear he expected me to make the decision. He was so accustomed to having other people make decisions for him that he still found it easier to let someone else decide what was going to happen next – as long, of course, as the decision didn't involve a young, lithe body and a cute smile.

'We'll think about it,' I told him, though I didn't have any money of my own and I would have certainly not recommended to Elvis that he put any of his money into such a dodgy undertaking. 'Meanwhile, what are you going to pay us for taking these papers to the distributor?'

'Take an extra two dozen copies of the paper and sell them in the street,' said the fat man, who didn't seem in the slightest bit surprised or disappointed that I hadn't shown more interest in investing in his newspaper. 'You can keep what you make. But you pay for the petrol you buy.'

'OK' I said. I stuffed the paper with the distributor's address on it into my jacket pocket and looked at Elvis. 'Let's start moving these papers downstairs,' I said.

Elvis looked at me and raised an eyebrow. 'If the Colonel could see me now!' he murmured so softly that only I heard him.

Chapter Thirty One

Elvis and I took half an hour to carry the newspapers downstairs and to the van. Only on my fourth journey did I manage to avoid either hitting my head or falling down the unexpected step. Hildy cheered me up a little by telling me that it took most people at least half a dozen visits to remember to duck down and to step down at the same time when coming into the offices, and to duck and step up when leaving. Elvis, being far the most graceful of us, neither hit his head nor missed the step after the first time.

It took us another hour to fill the van with the necessary fluids and to deliver the papers to the distributor's warehouse, which was situated a quarter of a mile or so away from the Cimetiere du Pere Lachaise on the outskirts of Paris.

`Give me the keys,' I told Elvis before we started out. `I'd better drive.'

`I like driving,' said Elvis, holding onto the keys and clearly unwilling to part with them.

`I don't think you'll like driving this heap,' I told him. `But this isn't about having fun.' I explained to him that neither of us had driving licences and neither of us was entitled to drive.

`So I'll take my chances,' said Elvis. `I'll drive carefully.'

`You're in Paris,' I pointed out. `Even if you drive like an old lady on her way to church there's still a good chance that someone else will hit us. Have you seen how the Parisians drive? And if you're driving when we're hit then we're going to be in trouble.'

I was not exaggerating. When French drivers get behind the wheel of a car they are interested in only three things: the accelerator, the ashtray and the horn. The first and third of these they press all the time. The ashtray they fill as quickly as possible. Despite this economy of interest French drivers really need three hands; one for their cigarette, one to fondle the knee of any woman within reach and one to make rude gestures to other drivers and pedestrians and to make the sign of the cross after near misses. French drivers steer with their knees. They would regard it as a waste of valuable resources to use their hands to hold the steering wheel.

Elvis didn't understand.

'If there's an accident they'll find that you don't have a licence. And then a trivial bump will probably turn into something rather more serious. There will be questions and more questions and they'll sit you in a room and stare at you. The chances of someone recognising you are considerably greater than the chances of anyone recognising me.' Suddenly, something else occurred to me. 'Have you ever been fingerprinted?'

'Yeah! I was printed back in the States. I had all these law enforcement badges. They did me then.' Elvis sounded quite proud about this. 'And I think they fingerprinted me when I was in Germany. I can't remember why but I seem to remember getting my fingers all inky. Some security thing, I guess.'

Elvis still didn't seem to be taking any of this seriously.

'If you're involved in an accident they'll find that you don't have a driving licence,' I reminded him again. 'Even in France, and given that the French drive motor cars the way drunken teenagers drive dodgem cars, that's bound to be some sort of offence. There's then a good chance they'll photograph and fingerprint you. All they've got to do then is match up the fingerprints and we're in serious, serious trouble.'

Elvis held out the keys to the van as though they'd suddenly become toxic and handed them to me.

I was right about driving the van not being much fun. I found that if I pressed the accelerator right down to the floor I could get the van up to a fast walking pace. The problem was that it took a long time to reach top speed. Every time I had to stop, for traffic lights or some other inconvenience, I had to fight my way through an unwilling gear box in order to claw my way back to cruising speed. I quickly gave up stopping, or even slowing down, for pedestrians. I found that the van was so slow that it was perfectly possible, and quite safe, to swerve around even the slowest of wayfarers brave enough to traverse a Parisian street.

We'd dropped off the 300 copies of the paper at the distributor's offices and were back in the Citroen when Elvis saw a sign for the famous Pere Lachaise cemetery.

'Isn't that where Jim Morrison is buried?' Elvis asked me.

'It is,' I confirmed. As far as I was aware Elvis had never even met Morrison and I don't think he had much time for the music of the Doors (though, like most professional musicians, Morrison had enormous respect for Elvis) and so I was impressed that he knew where he had died and where he was buried.

'I heard about him dying in Paris,' said Elvis. 'They say he was into drugs.'

'I believe so,' I said. Elvis never thought that the stuff he took counted as drugs. As far as he was concerned you weren't taking drugs unless you used a syringe, a needle and an illegal supplier.

'Let's go take a look,' said Elvis.

I found somewhere to park the Citroen and Elvis and I walked up into the cemetery. It's a massive place of over 100 acres and the cemetery is home to over a million people, including celebrities such as Oscar Wilde, Pierre Abelard and Heloise d'Argeneuil, Edith Piaf, Balzac, Colette, Modigliani, Proust, Moliere, Frederic Chopin and many more, but at the time Morrison was the resident most visitors wanted to see. His grave wasn't difficult to find. Even without the chalk arrows and messages crudely and irreverently drawn on other gravestones and mausoleums it was easy to find because of the smell of marijuana and cheap red wine. The grave was surrounded by hippies, smoking and drinking, and a bearded fellow was playing a guitar as though he'd only just bought it and didn't really know what it was for. A young couple were half sitting on the grave, kissing and fondling each other. I could see that Elvis was terribly upset at the irreverent way these so-called fans were behaving. He turned and walked away. I followed him, hurried a little, and caught up. I looked at him. There were tears rolling down his cheeks. I knew he was wondering if his own grave was being treated in a similar way.

We walked around the cemetery for a few minutes, reading the inscriptions on the gravestones. Some of the inscriptions were heartbreaking. An inconsolable man whose wife had died had engraved upon his wife's tomb the words: 'I am waiting to join her. Until I can join her I will simply keep myself occupied. She was loved by everyone whose lives she touched and she will live for ever in the hearts of those who knew her.'

Elvis stood and looked at it for a long, long time. Finally, he turned and walked slowly away. At the gate we passed a tramp. He wasn't begging but we both gave him some money. He told me that he slept in the Metro but came to Pere Lachaise every day because when he was there he was better off than the vast majority of the other inhabitants. 'It is,' he said, 'the only place in Paris where I can say this.' We walked back to the Citroen without saying another word. It was twenty minutes or so before Elvis spoke again.

'Let me make sure I understand these jobs you've got us,' said Elvis as we lurched our way back from Pere Lachaise. Citroen used to advertise their vehicles by showing a farmer drive over a ploughed field without breaking any of the eggs on his back seat. I don't know what had happened to the fat man's van but it didn't seem to have any springs at all. As a result driving along a perfectly ordinary Paris road was like driving across a ploughed field. 'We deliver newspapers, like a pair of 12-year-old boys except that we get to ride in an old van instead of on bicycles, and in return for our hard labour we are allowed to stand in the street and sell papers to people passing by. If we manage to sell any copies we can keep what we make. If we don't sell any papers then we're out the cost of the petrol we had to put into the van in order to make our delivery. Am I right so far?'

'That's pretty much it,' I agreed. A cyclist overtook us and used his left hand to express his contempt for our vehicle, our speed and my driving.

'And in our new role as ace investigative journalists we trudge around the hotels and small shops trying to persuade them to take copies of *The American in Paris?*'

'And to buy advertising,' I said. 'Don't forget we have the opportunity to sell advertising to the people who own the hotels, bars and tourist shops.'

Elvis shook his head and closed his eyes. It was, I suspected, quite a climb down. Even lorry driving was a step up from selling newspaper advertising to bars.

'It's a starting point,' I insisted, rather desperately.

The truth was that I didn't have the foggiest idea where else in Paris we could find work. Things weren't working out quite as I had intended. I'd rather imagined that finding work in Paris wouldn't be all that much of a challenge. But not having references, or any sort of a past, looked as if it might be more of a problem than I had imagined. 'If we get some good stories we can start writing for the paper. And once we know a bit more about the way it's all run we could perhaps think about investing in it.'

Elvis opened his eyes for a moment, looked at me, looked away and closed them again.

'The trouble is,' I said. 'We don't have any job history. We don't have any references. We don't have any qualifications which we can show to a prospective employer. The fact is that we're a bit stuffed.'

'I didn't think job hunting was going to be this hard,' said Elvis.

'But you don't have to find a job,' I reminded him. 'You've got money.'

'If you're working, then I'm working,' insisted Elvis. 'Maybe it'll be interesting.' He paused, opened his eyes, looked at me and grinned. 'It might even be fun.' He paused, clearly thinking, and then the smile came and the twinkle appeared in his eyes and I knew, without a moment of hesitation, what he was thinking. 'If we're going into shops and hotels,' he said, 'we're bound to meet loads of girls, right?'

It seemed to me that the new, streamlined Elvis would be happy as long as there were plenty of opportunities to meet members of the opposite sex. And, in Paris, there certainly seemed to be no shortage of those. Not as far as Elvis was concerned anyway.

When we got back to the building where *The American in Paris* lived, I parked the car in the courtyard where we'd found it and took the keys back upstairs to the fat man's office in the sky. I gave Elvis the two dozen copies of the paper we'd been given to sell and he said he'd take a look in a nearby Depot Vente shop to see if he could find a camera he liked.

There are Depot Vente shops all over Paris. They're a cross between antique shops and second hand shops, with the special difference being that all the stuff for sale has been put in the shop by its original owners. The people who run the Depot Vente make their profit by taking a percentage of the sale price. The Parisians use them a lot to buy furniture, household goods and things like cameras, torcheres, condiment sets, shotguns and all the other essentials for modern living in modern France. You can buy things you need, things you want and things you don't even know what they're for. Months later Elvis horrified me by announcing that on one visit to a Depot Vente store he had surreptitiously signed a pile of old Elvis albums and magazines which he'd seen for sale. 'No one will know whether or not the signatures are real,' he chuckled.

When I eventually got back down to street level I found Elvis leaning against the wall, waiting for me to return. He had a camera hanging from his neck but our two dozen newspapers had disappeared.

'Where have the papers gone?' I asked.

'I sold them.' He looked very pleased with himself.

'All of them?'

'All two dozen!' Elvis showed me a bundle of notes. 'At fifteen francs each it comes to 360 francs.'

I was impressed. Even allowing for the petrol and oil we'd had to buy for the van we'd made a decent profit.

'I sold them all to a coach load of Japanese tourists,' said Elvis. 'There was a traffic jam and their coach stopped for a moment. I got the driver to open the door, hopped on board and sold the lot. Easy, man.'

'Did they speak English?'

Elvis shrugged. 'Not that I know of.' He split the bundle into two and gave me one of the halves. We both stuffed the notes into our pockets.

It was, I realised, just another bizarre example of the legendary Elvis charm. If Elvis had decided to go into politics he would have been elected the world's first President. And the appointment would have been for life. Those who met him claim that John F. Kennedy was charismatic. But not for one second do I believe that Kennedy was in Elvis's league. Elvis had unprecedented talent and impressive professional skills but those weren't the virtues that had turned him into the world's most successful performer.

He had natural charm without boundaries and a presence that cannot be learned or acquired. When he walked into a room the place lit up. Everyone noticed. Men stood a little taller in order not to disappear completely in his shadow. And women pushed out their chests and made all the unconscious movements women make in order to be noticed by the rooster in the room. There will never be as big a star as Elvis was in his heyday – not until we have a world government and a single television channel.

'I thought we could celebrate the sale with a couple of vin chauds!' said Elvis. There's a café on the corner.' In Paris there is always a café on the corner. There are more cafés in Paris than there are traffic wardens in any other city. It is sometimes hard to see how they all stay in business. But they do. The French in general, and the Parisians in particular, regard cafés as an integral part of life, just as essential as wine, sex and shouting at motorists. Look into any café in the early morning and you'll see workmen in overalls standing side by side at the bar with businessmen in smart suits, all starting the day by fortifying themselves with a brandy or a glass of wine. They'll be there again in the evening, having a couple of drinks; the first to reward themselves for surviving another day and the second to prepare themselves for the journey home. Elvis bent down and picked up something that he'd put down behind him. He tried to do it sneakily, so that I didn't notice.

I looked down to see what else he had acquired. 'What's that?' I asked, unnecessarily. I was horrified and could hardly believe my eyes.

'It's a Nikon!' he said. 'I have one of these back at Graceland. Great. Easy to use. Good pictures. I've got a Canon too.' And then, when he realised what he'd said, there was a painful pause. He looked uncomfortable for a moment. 'Had one of these,' he said, correcting himself. Everything he'd left behind at Graceland was now part of his past and nothing to do with his present or his future.

I didn't want to put him on the spot because I felt sorry for him over the Graceland slip. But as we set off for the café I had to ask him. 'What else did you buy?'

Elvis blushed a little. He hummed and hawed for a moment but didn't reply.

'What's in the guitar case that you're trying to hide?' I asked. I knew, of course. And Elvis knew that I knew. And I knew that he knew that I knew. But, and I don't really know why, I wanted him to tell me.

Elvis looked at me and switched on the smile: the full, 100 watt smile that he kept for women and special occasions.

'It's a guitar,' he said. 'I bought myself a guitar.'

He did, I remember, have the good grace to look guilty.

'It was a bargain,' he added. 'It was really cheap. I thought maybe I could do a little busking. Maybe in a park. Or perhaps I could go down into the Metro.'

I looked at him and raised an eyebrow. Elvis had never been down in the Paris underground in his life. I doubt if he knew how to get there.

'It might bring us in a few francs,' he said. 'I could busk outside that new museum.'

'The Centre Pompidou?'

Paris's latest museum had opened a few months earlier. The British architect had put the building's infrastructure, including piping, on the outside of the building, even the escalators ran up the outside, and the museum was still the talk of Paris. The new mayor of Paris, a young and thrusting politician called Jacques Chirac, had been on Pompidou's staff when he'd been President of France. It was certainly a fact that buskers who worked the area in front of the museum seemed to do well.

'That's the one,' agreed Elvis.

I thought about this for a moment and then nodded my head slightly.

'And it would probably be a bit of fun.'

I knew what he was thinking. I knew what he meant by a 'bit of fun'. Long legs, cute smiles and innocence in between. Elvis didn't want to busk in order to earn the price of a meal, or a cup of coffee. He missed the crowd of willing girls who had hung around outside his door wherever he had been and who had thrown themselves at him long before the word 'groupie' had been coined. He hoped, I suspected, that playing the guitar again would prove to be just as much a draw for his new identity as it had been for the old one.

We were still sitting in the café he had spotted. It was the sort of café which is patronised by locals rather than tourists and we each had a large glass of hot, red, spiced wine in front of us. In the smaller, cheaper, less fashionable cafés the patron always serves vin chaud in much bigger glasses. In the cafés next to busy street markets, where the customers are largely workmen who've either been humping huge baskets of fruit and vegetables around or standing in the cold haggling with customers over the price of a bunch of bananas or a couple of cabbages, the stuff is served in half litre tumblers. A drink that is a fashionable table accessory at the Café de la Paix, Lipps or Deux Magot becomes a quick and extremely pleasant way to get tiddly in a café or bar where most of the customers are wearing blue overalls.

'If you start singing in a park it won't be five minutes before someone spots that you're the real thing,' I warned him. 'No impersonator, not even the professional ones, manages to get the voice just right. And even with the moustache, and the short hair and the contact lenses you still look too much like Elvis to get away with it.'

'Maybe, if I just played the guitar?'

'And didn't sing?'

'And didn't sing,' Elvis agreed. 'I'll be a solo instrumentalist.'

I thought about it.

'You can't play any of your own songs,' I told him. I hated the idea of him playing music in public but I knew how much of a buzz he'd got from performing. I knew he missed having an audience hanging onto his every move, watching his every gesture. An average Elvis audience consisted largely of women who would have happily left their homes, their husbands, their children, their lives, their everything for a night with their idol. No, forget that. For an hour alone with their idol. Women who would, afterwards, have regretted nothing. The much admired Sun King, his glorious majesty Louis X1V of France, would have envied Elvis his hold over his subjects.

'I don't know much else!'

'Then you'll have to learn something.'

'OK. I'll buy some new music.'

I assured him that there were good music shops in the region around the Boulevard Saint Michel and promised that we'd go there and hunt out some blues or gospel tunes which I hoped he could play without turning the centre of Paris into a huge traffic jam. I couldn't begin to imagine the size of the crowds that would gather if word got out that Elvis Presley was singing 'Blue Suede Shoes' in the Jardin du Luxembourg.

'But meanwhile,' I said, 'we have to decide if we're going to go ahead and try to get something going with Hildy's newspaper.'

Elvis was far more enthusiastic than I'd expected him to be. Selling our allotted bundle of newspapers to a coach full of Japanese tourists had convinced him that we could make some money and build ourselves the beginnings of a future. Neither of us trusted Hildebrand, the fat man who owned and ran the paper, but to be honest we didn't have too many other alternatives on offer.

Chapter Thirty Two

The next week or two went by fairly quickly. We soon established some sort of routine. Every Wednesday afternoon we took Hildy's terrible little van to the printers in the 17th arrondissement and picked up the latest edition of *The American in Paris*. We dropped just under half of these at the distributors which were, although still in Paris, about as far away from the printers as was possible, and took the remainder to the offices in the Rue Bonaparte.

It was Elvis who realised that we really didn't have to carry all those bundles of newspapers up the stairs to Hildy's offices to be stored, and then carry them all the way back down again when we were ready to sell them, but that we could just leave them locked in the back of the Citroen and use the vehicle as a sort of mobile warehouse. We pooh poohed our employer's fear that a crook might steal both the van and the week's print run by pointing out that no self-respecting car thief would be seen dead stealing such a rickety and unreliable contraption, and the chances of anyone wanting to steal a couple of thousand copies of *The American in Paris* were slimmer still.

It took us a week to persuade Hildy to accept one of our news stories for publication in the paper. Purely by accident, Elvis spotted a film location scout he recognised. Heaven knows where he'd met him because to the best of my knowledge Elvis had never hung out with location scouts, casting directors, grips or even cameramen when he'd been making films. He liked mixing with stunt guys and chorus girls but that was about it. We were buying English and American publications at the W.H.Smith bookshop in the Rue de Rivoli when Elvis suddenly nudged me and pointed the guy out to me. He didn't know the fellow's name but he had a fairly unforgettable face and a beard that made him look like Rasputin, the mad Russian monk.

`I hope you don't mind my bothering you,' I said, `but I recognise you. I must have seen your picture somewhere. You're a location scout for the movies, aren't you?'

The man looked delighted and flattered. 'There was a small picture of me in Variety a couple of months ago,' he said. 'Perhaps you saw that?' People who work on the fringes of show business and who are accustomed to being ignored and over-looked, are terribly quick to succumb to a chance to sparkle for a moment.

'That must have been it,' I agreed quickly.

Within minutes the guy had told me that he was doing preliminary scouting work for a proposed Woody Allen movie and that if things went well Woody would be filming in Paris the following year. He readily agreed to be interviewed and was so thrilled to be facing the business end of a camera for a change that I didn't think there was a chance in a million that he would notice, let alone recognise, the man who was taking the pictures.

I managed to extract 1,500 words from this fairly trivial event and Elvis took half a dozen pictures of the guy posing in possible film locations. We even managed to have the mighty location scout photographed outside bars and hotels where we were trying to sell copies of the paper. The owners or managers promised to take copies on sale or return if the pictures appeared in the paper. I exaggerated slightly and told them the scout was an important Hollywood producer and that if things went well they could find themselves looking after a film crew with someone else's money to squander. 'Paul Newman stay here?' asked one of the managers. I nodded. 'Steve McQueen?' I nodded again. He grinned broadly and took thirty copies of *The American In Paris* on sale or return. He had no idea, of course, that the man with his cap on backwards, busily taking the photographs, had been a bigger star than either of them.

Hildy was surprised and thrilled when we showed him the feature we'd produced and he immediately allocated it a double page spread early in the next week's edition. He even agreed to pay us in real money instead of simply giving us a bundle of papers to sell. I don't think he had really believed that we were ever likely to bring him any genuine editorial.

Up until that point nearly all the stuff that appeared in *The American in Paris* had been produced by Hildy's one contributor, Gerald, an ageing former employee of the 'International Herald Tribune' whose fondness for alcohol in almost any form explained why most of the pictures printed in the paper seemed sharp to him but slightly blurred to everyone else. Gerald, who had a substantial personal allowance from a former wife whose father had made his money from selling hamburgers and fries to families all over the American mid-west, was delighted to find that he could spend more time drinking and less time struggling to remember where he'd left his camera and why he was where he was. Elvis's pictures were a damned sight better than anything that had been published in the paper for years and the abdicated King of Rock'n'Roll even used a small amount of his unlimited charm to persuade a seemingly endless series of waitresses, receptionists and shop girls from the city's bars, hotels and emporia to unfasten the top buttons of their blouses just enough to add a little natural cleavage to the paper's photographs. He had, of course, obtained all the telephone numbers of those who were pretty and under 25-years-old. Elvis had never been shy about pursuing female companionship, nor about converting a passing acquaintanceship into a close relationship in the shortest possible time, but it was now perfectly clear that his success in this area had never been as dependent upon his rock star status as uninformed observers might have believed. The only significant difference was that he now had to spend a little more time talking, charming and smiling than had hitherto been the case.

Naturally, we found that the two halves of our side of the newspaper business helped each other. Hoteliers were keen to tell us if they had important Americans staying with them because I always mentioned both the establishment and the manager by name. And after Elvis had taken a few photographs they were usually willing to take a dozen copies of the paper to display on their reception counter. Finding news and feature stories helped us to sell papers and trying to sell papers helped us find stories to use in the paper.

Occasionally, we came across big stars purely because we happened to be in the right place at the right time. We were talking to a concierge in a famous Paris hotel when he leant towards us and whispered, in a conspiratorial style, that film star Robert de Niro had just left the hotel. Elvis and I hung around in the lobby for three hours before de Niro returned. I didn't manage to get an interview but Elvis snatched several excellent photographs which we were able to use. Hildy was delighted and the hotel manager didn't seem to mind the publicity.

'Do you miss it?' I asked Elvis afterwards.
'Miss what?'

`Being the big star. Having people rush to take photographs of you.'

Elvis grinned and shook his head. `Been there, done that.'

I believed him too. He never seemed envious or sad about the fact that he had walked away from superstardom. I think the simple truth was that he had become such a huge star, and such a genuine legend, that the accompanying fuss and razzmatazz had crushed his own personality. He'd been stifled by stardom so totally that he didn't ever want to go back. He genuinely enjoyed the freedom that his new life gave him. We weren't earning much money from the newspaper, certainly not enough for both of us to live on, but things were getting better, we still had quite a chunk of the cash we'd brought to Paris and the diamonds were still in the ice tray of our refrigerator. If things went quiet and there weren't any real stars around we created a few of our own. We'd talk to prosperous looking foreigners and, with very little help from us, they would happily feed us useable bullshit by the wagon load. A shirt manufacturer from Idaho agreed that he was planning to open a factory in Paris and boasted that, as a direct result, most French shirt manufacturers would be facing bankruptcy within eighteen months. It was the sort of jingoistic story American visitors lapped up. No one becomes more patriotic than a traveller temporarily exiled from their homeland, and American tourists who had just been ripped off by tour guides and sneered at by taxi drivers and waiters were only too ready to hear that an American businessman was planning corporate revenge.

A plump and giggly woman from Washington D.C., who wore a dress which took décolleté to new depths, boasted that her sober and dull looking new husband was certain to be the next American Ambassador to France. We took pictures of the two honeymooners sitting in the bar at their hotel just off the Champs Élysées. The husband tried to talk down his wife's expectations but quickly backtracked when she expressed surprise at his lack of confidence and made it clear that the boast had originated with him. We managed to obtain a weekly order for four dozen newspapers from the manager of the hotel. We didn't offer him the opportunity to return unsold newspapers so these were firm sales and money in the bank. A disk jockey from Texas told us that when he got back home he was going to devote an entire radio show to Johnny Hallyday and other French rockers. He insisted that with his help Monsieur Hallyday would become a bigger star than Elvis Presley and posed for photographs holding a clutch of bestselling albums recorded by the French star. His hotel manager ordered a weekly supply of six newspapers but upped this to twelve when Elvis took a picture of him posing with the disc jockey and pointing to a poster promoting a Johnny Hallyday concert which decorated a nearby Morris pillar. (These cylindrical advertising columns appear all over Paris and are named after a printer called Gabriel Morris who held the concession for advertising on them back in 1868. Every few years local politicians talk about getting rid of them but the inevitable fury means that they remain while the politicians usually disappear.)

And I confess that, just occasionally, when there wasn't even any half-news around, we weren't beyond creating news and feature stories of our own. It was, inevitably perhaps, Hildy who suggested that we blur the boundaries between fact and fiction.

'You haven't got much this week,' he complained, one Tuesday afternoon.

'There isn't much happening,' I replied.

'You mean you haven't found out what's happening,' retorted our esteemed editor and publisher.

'We've spoken to all the hotel people we know,' I protested. 'There are no stars in town this week. The hotels are full of carburettor salesmen and holiday-makers from Idaho.'

'So, use your imaginations!' said Hildy. 'Liven things up a bit!' He glared at me and, seeing that I didn't understand, added: 'Make some stuff up!'

At first I was reluctant to taint my quaint journalistic morals by creating news reports which had only tenuous links to the truth but when I thought about it the moral arguments rather faded away. After all, our whole life was a fraud. I had been responsible for creating the biggest fake story in the history of journalism. How much more harm could I possibly do to my image of myself as a fearless, truth seeking journalist?

I wrote a story claiming that Muhammad Ali had been seen dining at Fouquet's on the Champs Élysées and suggested that Ali was planning a second title fight against British boxer Joe Bugner. Naturally, I quoted an unnamed source who said that the fight would be held in Paris. I quoted unnamed sources as claiming that an eminent American boxing impresario was trying to obtain permission for the Ali-Bugner fight to be held in an open air arena in the shadow of the Eiffel Tower. We illustrated this entirely spurious story with photographs of the back of a tall, broad shouldered black man leaving Fouquet's in a tweed overcoat and a flat cap. A photograph of the Eiffel Tower completed the feature.

For the following week's paper Elvis and I produced an illustrated feature claiming that Michael Jackson was staying at the Ritz Hotel in Paris. Elvis took photographs of an unidentified top floor window and I wrote an entirely fake interview with an inevitably anonymous hotel employee who explained how Jackson had been smuggled into and out of the hotel through the kitchens and the service lift. I suspect that people believed this story because nothing about it was unbelievable. We found a hospital worker who had been on duty when a still young Maria Callas had died of a heart attack in Paris. The hospital worker, down on her luck and happy to talk to us for a few francs, gave us a dramatic first person account of what had happened. Callas had died just a month after Elvis's official death.

No one was hurt by any of this nonsense. Indeed, as far as we could tell, everyone gained. We always made it clear that we were discussing rumours rather than facts and the principals referred to in our stories received a little local publicity which could not possibly have done them any harm. And Hildy certainly didn't object. He would have been happy to run a sports story reporting that Vlad the Impaler had defeated Attila the Hun in a thrilling five set tennis match at the Roland Garros stadium if we'd been able to provide him with half convincing quotes from two awestruck spectators. After making up stories for a few weeks I eventually understood why tabloid writers are paid much higher salaries than journalists who work for broadsheet newspapers. The simple fact is that writing for tabloids and supermarket publications requires far more imagination. You have to be creative to make up really convincing quotes.

From time to time our stories attracted attention from bigger newspapers, and from television and radio stations in America and Britain as well as around Europe. An entirely imaginative story in which we reported that Faye Dunaway had been seen dining with Francois Truffaut at the George V hotel just off the Champs Élysées led to an international feeding frenzy. A journalist working for a newspaper in Rome wrote an article suggesting that Truffaut was planning to cast Dunaway as Madame Bovary in a new film version of Flaubert's masterpiece. And a story which reported that former American President Gerald Ford had been seen shopping in the Rue St Honore and in the Samaritain store next to the Pont Neuf led a British commentator to suggest that Ford was planning a move to Paris. Naturally, we were unable to illustrate our story with any photographs of President Ford but it wasn't difficult to find shop assistants who were happy to claim that they'd seen him picking out bed linen and living room furniture. Both Elvis and I were amused when British politicians joined the publicity bandwagon by asking why a former American President should choose to move to France rather than to England. 'Is this the end of the 'special' relationship'?' asked a clearly offended former cabinet minister in a 2,000 word article in a broadsheet newspaper.

Chapter Thirty Three

Hildy, our plump employer, was pleased with the effect all these stories were having on the paper's circulation but all three of us knew that in order to keep the circulation rising we had to keep finding (or `creating') good news and feature stories. Our biggest problem was that we had a very small regular readership. Most of our readers were only in Paris for one or two issues and when they'd left their hotels and gone back home we had to sell the newspaper to an entirely new bunch of customers. We were forever re-launching the paper to an entirely new audience. It was painfully obvious that if we were to produce a genuine, permanent increase in the circulation we would have to increase the size of the regular readership. We needed stories and features which appealed to Americans and Britons who lived in Paris, rather than those who were just visiting for a short stay.

In order to try to increase the regular readership Hildy decided to increase the amount of space devoted to clubs, discotheques and theatres. We all agreed that if the paper contained more reviews of what was happening in the Paris music scene we might be able to attract some English speaking Parisians as well as American and British expatriates living in the city. We chose to specialise in the music scene rather than any other form of entertainment because neither I nor Elvis understood French well enough to be able to review a play, music hall or comedian. My rusty French was getting better, and Elvis could order a meal, buy a shirt or chat up a waitress, but there's a huge gap between being able to cope with simple day to day conversations and being able to understand what's being said by fast talking actors and comedians. A hugely successful Paris concert by Pink Floyd had really woken up the Parisian music lovers and new bands were appearing almost nightly, while the world's biggest acts now had Paris right on the top of their `must visit' venue list. Both Bob Dylan and the band Queen had enjoyed hugely successful gigs at the Pavilion de Paris.

Not surprisingly, Elvis had some initial difficulty coping with our visits to the clubs, particularly when, as sometimes happened, we found ourselves interviewing singers or musicians who had an exceptionally high regard for their own talents and status in the music world.

There was, for example, one awful evening when we found ourselves interviewing a rock and roll band whose lead singer had based his performance almost entirely on Elvis's own. His stance on his stage, his hip movements and his mannerisms were all taken straight out of the Elvis Presley stage handbook. And he and his band played virtually nothing but Elvis Presley classics.

The singer was supercilious, patronising and immensely self-important. He made us wait three quarters of an hour for an interview, even though he wasn't doing anything other than drink beer with the other band members. When he finally condescended to see us I asked him if he regarded himself as a tribute singer or an Elvis impersonator. It was a genuine question, meant without malice, but he took immediate offence and became extremely aggressive and abusive. When he began complaining that Elvis had been just lucky, and that his career had been created by a posse of media friendly journalists, I closed my notebook and suggested to Elvis that he should put away his camera and we should leave. It was fortunate, at the time, that Elvis didn't understand enough French to know precisely what the wannabe singer was saying.

Far more embarrassing was the evening we spent at a small club in the Rue Saint Andre des Arts in the 5th arrondissement. Apart from a small entrance lobby on the ground floor, the club was, like the Cavern in Liverpool, entirely underground. There were usually three or four acts on stage during a single evening's show and the night we were there the last of the four bands to perform was called 'Jimmy et les Assistants'. ('Assistant' is the French for 'wizard' and so the band's name wasn't quite so bad as it seemed in English). They played pleasant enough rock'n'roll, most of it 1960's stuff, but neither the band nor the individual musicians seemed particularly talented. I remember that they all wore black lipstick and had golden moons and stars stuck to their faces. They were dressed in the sort of capes and pointed hats usually associated with wizards and the cheapest sort of magicians and I thought they seemed rather juvenile and silly to be honest. They looked and sounded more like a group of very amateurish medical students having a bit of fun than a professional band trying to claw their way up the ladder to a recording contract, a spot on French television and at a gig at Olympia, Bercy or some other major venue.

We'd watched them strum and batter their way through a few Buddy Holly classics, a couple of Bobby Darin favourites and a pretty awful version of 'Heartbreak Hotel' when a girl I vaguely recognised appeared at our table and sat down on the only empty chair.

'They are fantastic, no?' she said. It was very noisy and she had to shout to make herself heard.

It was only then that I recognised her. She was the waitress who had spent the night with Elvis after he'd picked her up in a café.

'Hello, Dominique!' said Elvis, who was clearly as surprised as I was to see her.

We talked, or rather shouted, for a while and she told us that Jimmy, the lead singer of the band, was her boyfriend. She then asked us how we'd heard of the band.

Elvis showed her his camera and I explained that we were working for a newspaper and planning to write a review of the bands which had appeared.

Dominique was very excited by this and immediately insisted that at the end of the gig we should meet Jimmy and his 'assistants' and write a special feature about them. 'You must photograph them before they take off their make-up and costumes,' she told Elvis. 'It is our plan that they will never be photographed in any other way.'

Out of politeness more than pleasure we stayed for the rest of the set and then followed Dominique back stage. She introduced us to Jimmy and the rest of the band (whose names I have, I'm afraid, long forgotten) and told them that we were journalists working for an important American newspaper. She didn't mention the fact that she had met us both before and I remember being thankful for this. For one awful moment, as we struggled along a narrow, stone corridor to the group's tiny dressing room, I had wondered if Dominique intended to introduce Elvis as a former lover of hers.

'We're the hottest band in France,' boasted Jimmy when we'd been introduced. I nodded and resisted the temptation to ask him why, if they were so 'hot', they were sharing the bill with three other bands and working in a club which, even when crammed to the walls, couldn't possibly accommodate more than sixty or seventy music hungry patrons.

'I hate Americans,' said the drummer, who emphasised this remark by spitting on the floor. He, like the rest of the band, was swigging French beer from a bottle. No one offered Elvis or myself a drink.

'He just says that because he thinks it is controversial and will make him famous,' whispered Dominique.

The band's manager, a particularly rancid looking Frenchman who wore a cheap suit that was several sizes too big for him, asked if we were going to pay to interview the band. He had a ring of hair around his skull and other than this was completely bald. He had a hooked nose, his left heel tapped constantly on the floor and every few seconds he sniffed as though he had a cold and really needed to blow his nose.

I looked at him as though he were completely mad and told him that if he didn't want us to do the interview we would quite happily leave. I asked him if he knew where we could find the other acts. One of the other bands, the second to appear, had seemed quite promising. They had played several original songs and they'd looked much better than any of the other bands.

'No, no, no,' insisted the manager, suddenly changing his mind about wanting a fee. 'You must stay here with us.' He pulled a small plastic bag out of his jacket pocket and offered the bag first to me and then to Elvis. The bag contained a number of red and black capsules. I had no idea what they were. We both declined, politely.

'I'm going to be bigger than Johnny,' said Jimmy. He paused and thought for a moment. 'Bigger than Elvis.' He seemed to have forgotten that he was actually a member of a band and not a solo singer. 'I'm going to do something with my life. I don't want to be a mere spectator, like you people.'

'Jolly good,' I said, as the real Elvis snapped away with his camera. Elvis had become an excellent photographer and was now taking terrific pictures. He was particularly good at taking moody pictures which looked good in black and white on a newspaper page. Back in the 1970's many photographers were so taken with the delights of colour film that they forgot that newspapers needed pictures in black and white.

'Do you have any original material?' I asked.

'We will consider material offered to us by song writers,' said the amazingly arrogant Jimmy.

'You don't write any of your own?'

Jimmy shook his head. 'We are musicians not writers,' he said, with a sneer.

'How would you describe yourself and the band?' I asked him. 'Sum up your appeal in three words.'

'Sexy, sexy, sexy,' said Jimmy immediately. He put his arm around Dominique's waist. 'We already have plenty of groupies like this one.'

Dominique blushed, clearly embarrassed if not humiliated, and I felt rather angry on her behalf. She looked as if she were about to cry.

'We share them around,' said Jimmy, clearly quite unaware that Dominique was upset. He gave her a pat on the behind in a proprietorial sort of way. She seemed out of place and out of her depth.

'I've got enough,' said Elvis quietly, putting the lens cap back on his camera. I'd heard that he hadn't always been Sir Galahad as far as groupies were concerned but even he seemed unimpressed by Jimmy's manner. And maybe he felt sorry for Dominique. She had, after all, been his first girl since he had started his new life in France.

We asked a few more bread and butter questions. Names, ages and so on, and then we left. Dominique followed us back up the stairs.

'He thinks he must behave like a big rock star,' she said. I turned and noticed her quietly wiping tears from her eyes. 'It is very smoky in there,' she explained. 'It makes my eyes water sometimes.'

'Maybe if he could learn a little humility he might be more successful,' said Elvis gently. 'It doesn't hurt to be polite to people. In public at least.' We had reached the top of the stairs. I opened the door. It was well after midnight but the street outside was still bright and busy with people.

Dominique looked at Elvis and shook her head. 'That's not the way the music business works,' she said. 'To succeed you must be tough, nasty, ruthless with everyone around you.'

'That's not true,' said Elvis, quietly.

'I'm afraid you do not understand,' said Dominique sternly. 'To understand these things you have to be in the music business. It is different for them.'

Elvis struggled for a moment but said nothing.

'Sure,' I said. 'Good luck. I hope they make it.'

Elvis and I knew they wouldn't.

And, deep down, I think Dominique thought they wouldn't either.

For her sake I wrote a pleasant 300 word piece about the band and the paper printed a couple of good pictures.

I have no idea what subsequently happened to any of the band members and their enthusiastic advocate.

I hope Dominique found a decent, faithful husband; preferably someone who worked in a bank or an estate agency, played football on Sunday afternoons and gave her 2.4 children and a cute dog, of assorted sexes. I suspect the gloriously untalented band members spent their working lives doing something outside show business; always ready to talk about how their tentative grasp on superstardom was smashed by the cruel overlords of an unfeeling and insensitive music industry.

Chapter Thirty Four

We didn't spend all our time working, of course. Since we were planning on the city being our permanent home I wanted Elvis to get to know Paris, and we needed to find a better apartment. The one I'd selected for the first few weeks of our life in Paris was fine as a short-term solution but we agreed that we really needed to be on the other side of the Champs de Mars, closer to the centre of the city. And, if we could find somewhere affordable, we needed somewhere a little larger. We also had to decide whether we should rent or buy. Elvis was keen to buy somewhere. `I felt comfortable at Graceland because I owned it,' he said. `My parents always lived in rentals or public housing. Graceland was a big step. It was the first time in my life that I didn't have to worry about a landlord coming round.' I understood his feeling but didn't have the money to purchase an apartment. Elvis pointed out that he would be able to buy one with the money we would realise from the sale of the diamonds. I said he would but that if he did so I intended to pay him rent. It seemed to me that my self-respect, and our relationship, would only survive if I paid my way.

    We spent many happy hours just wandering around the city. We visited the well-known tourist sites, of course. But we also spent a good deal of time exploring the back streets and alleys of Paris. And Elvis was thrilled when I first showed him one of Paris's arcades.

    The passageways and arcades which criss-cross Paris are among the city's best kept secrets. I know Parisians who've lived in the city all their lives but who haven't ever bothered to find them. And many guidebooks ignore them completely. There are numerous glass roofed arcades or passages all over the city, most of them dating back to the 19th century or beyond, but the longest, brightest and best and most fun are probably the ones which head north and south from the Boulevard Montmartre in the 2nd arrondissement. The Passage Jouffroy heads north and the Passage de Panoramas goes south. These passageways all contain numerous tiny boutiques and cafés and are, of course, perfect for browsing on a rainy day. The Jouffroy even contains its own hotel (The Hotel Chopin) which has been there since the passage was founded in 1882.

All these passageways and arcades still give an exquisite sense of their former glory. Some of the arcades are quite short, but most are packed with surprises. We found that the Passage Verdeau, for example, was full of treasure-trove shops. The entrances to many of these arcades are often half hidden between shops or office buildings but once you know where they are it is possible to walk much of the way across Paris without going outside. On a cold and wet wintry day a trip along the passageways is a perfect way to go for a long walk without getting cold or wet. Elvis and I still visit the passageways and arcades and they've hardly changed in nearly four decades. Believe it or not we still see shopkeepers and waiters there who we recognise from our first visits.

We spent a good deal of time in the student quarter, the area of the left bank which lies on the opposite side of the river to Notre Dame. We became regular customers at a bookshop called Shakespeare & Company which is named after, but nothing to do with, the wonderful bookshop run by the legendary Sylvia Beach (the bookseller who first published Ulysses by James Joyce). The modern version of Shakespeare and Company was founded by George Whitman, a relative of Walt's, and it is a fascinating treasure trove of new and second hand books. (Like all great men, George's uncle, the American poet Walt Whitman wanted to be remembered for saying something profound and witty on his deathbed. He prepared a few bon mots for his final moment and whenever he thought he was dying he would utter something deeply moving and yet suitably succinct and memorable. But things didn't go according to plan. The last words of Walt Whitman, spoken to his valet Horace Traubel, were: 'Lift me up, Horace. I want to shit.')

We also visited the Hotel Dieu, the oldest hospital in the world, which is just a few paces from Notre Dame. The hospital was designed in an era when doctors still believed that patients benefitted from fresh air, gentle exercise and the sight and smell of flowers. The hospital is, therefore, built around a central courtyard and there are long cloisters along which recovering and convalescent patients can sit or stroll and listen to the birds whatever the weather. The hospital hasn't always been so attractive. A man we met there told us that a report published in 1788 described how patients were crammed six to a bed. Linen and used bandages were washed in the Seine which must have been fun for those downstream who took their drinking water from the river.

One Thursday afternoon we visited the famous Paris stamp market, held near the bottom of the Champs Élysées, and Elvis immediately recognised it as the site where the 1963 film `Charade' had been filmed. Cary Grant and Audrey Hepburn are looking for something valuable when they suddenly realise that the `something' they are searching for is an apparently worthless old stamp stuck on an envelope. The stamp is accidentally sold to a dealer on the market, allowing the stars to begin a desperate race against time. Elvis was greatly taken by the fact that the market looked just as it had in the film and ever after he was always on the look-out for bits and pieces of Paris which he recognised from the movies.

In addition to selling stamps, the dealers who have stalls there also sell old postcards and letters from the 19th century. Elvis, an incurable romantic, bought old Valentine's Day postcards which had been written and posted back in the 19th century. Amazingly, you could buy these for just a few centimes each. We chatted to the stall holders and improved our French. The Parisians, who can be very proprietorial and protective of their language, often corrected our pronunciation and our grammar, but, with a little sign language and a few words of English tossed in where we were unsure of the French equivalent, we could invariably make ourselves understood.

(Curiously, the French, who invariably speak English with atrocious accents and a complete disregard for the rules of grammar, are greatly offended if English speakers dare to offer advice.)

And as we wandered back from the stamp market we walked along the avenue Montaigne where many of the big fashion houses have their shops and display rooms. There are more couturiers and de-lux labels here than there are in Bond Street, London or Madison Avenue, New York. Elvis was impressed when I told him that the world of haute couture in Paris was founded not by a Frenchman but by an Englishman called Charles Frederick Worth. Mr Worth was invited to design clothes for the Empress Eugenie, the wife of Napoleon III, and to protect his designs he founded the Chambre Syndicale de la Haute Couture. Elvis and I had great fun looking in the shop windows, trying to find the most absurdly overpriced items. It is possible to find shops selling shoes, handbags and lingerie at eye watering prices. Not all that long ago Elvis had himself been the sort of customer these shops delighted in welcoming. Today, he laughed as he realised how absurdly expensive they were. We stood outside a shop which specialised in selling lingerie which would have been cheaper if it had been made of thick gold leaf. 'Have you noticed,' asked Elvis, 'how some women wear bras which maximise and exaggerate their breasts, while other women, better endowed by nature, wear bras which are specially designed to hide the fact that they have the breasts the women in the first group are pretending they have.' He shook his head and thought for a while about this. 'Whichever ever way you look at it,' he said, 'it's all fakery.'

And, of course, we wandered up into the 18th arrondissement, where the ghosts of Picasso, Matisse and Utrillo still sit and paint. The 18th contains Sacre Coeur, the place du Tetre and many miles of fascinating little alleyways, passages and stairways. There are steep, narrow winding streets, long flights of stone steps with ancient metal handrails and scores of small, wonderful restaurants and smoky bars. Sacre Coeur is dismissed by many as looking too much like a wedding cake. But that, we decided, is precisely why it is so appealing. The church dominates the northern skyline of Paris and the pavement in front of it provides the very best panoramic view of Paris. Occasionally, if there are no policemen in sight, there will be buskers working there. Curiously, the acoustics are fantastic and just about everything played sounds magnificent. A tone deaf man playing a tambourine would probably sound good.

It was here, on the pavement overlooking the rest of Montmartre, that Elvis first did a little busking. Naturally, I'd made him promise not to sing or play any of the songs which had made him famous. I was terrified that someone would recognise him. He'd bought a couple of books of guitar music and I remember he played 'Dock of the Bay', 'Down on the Corner', 'Bad Moon Rising' and one or two Beatles songs. Not surprisingly, I suppose, the busking went well. The scariest moment came when a couple of American tourists wanted to know if he knew any Elvis songs. He apologised and shrugged, suggesting that he didn't understand. The couple wandered off disappointed. After three quarters of an hour or so we were moved on by a surprisingly friendly gendarme but when we picked all the coins out of Elvis's guitar case we found that he'd earned nearly 70 francs. It may not have been Las Vegas style money but it was honestly earned and Elvis was as proud as a cat with new kittens. After this Elvis started busking regularly at various places in the city. He stuck to his promise not to sing but once or twice he snuck one or two of his own favourites into one of these busking gigs. He once held a bunch of Japanese tourists mesmerised with a guitar solo version of 'Love Me Tender'. They couldn't understand why he didn't start singing and eventually several members of the group sang the vocals while Elvis played guitar. It must have been terribly difficult for him. Only once did a passer-by give me an uneasy moment. 'If you put on fifty pounds, shaved off your moustache and grew sideburns you'd look like Elvis Presley,' a Canadian woman in her thirties told him. 'Oh, I don't think so,' said her husband. 'His eyes are the wrong colour and his nose looks different to me.'

We spent days wandering aimlessly along the Rue St Honore and the Rue de Rivoli where there are many excellent shops and as we walked around the place de la Concorde noticed many plaques commemorating the resistance fighters who died defending their city during the German occupation. Discrete, rectangular wall plaques with the words 'Ice est tombe' are to be found on almost every corner. Inevitably, there are many sad stories behind these plaques. Many people died in the last minutes of the occupation. The leader of the German command, Dietrich von Choltitz defied Hitler's orders to destroy Paris and refused to give the order to ignite the explosives which had been placed under all the city's landmarks, including Notre Dame and the Eiffel Tower. But he did tell his men to fight until their cartridges ran out. A French tank commander called Pierre Laigle, having just made his way into Paris, stopped to find a telephone so that he could ring the fiancée he hadn't seen or heard from in four years. Thrilled she set off to meet him but before she could make the rendezvous a German sniper, hiding in the Ministere de la Marine on the place de la Concorde, shot and killed him.

We had just walked past the Ritz Hotel in the Place Vendome one day when we had the scare of our lives. It suddenly seemed as though the whole of Paris was running in our direction. We both thought at that moment that Elvis had been spotted, his modest disguise penetrated. We froze as a screaming mob headed in our direction, alerted by a shout from the far distance and racing down the Avenue de l'Opera as though running away from a pride of hungry lions. But they weren't running away from anything and their faces were full of excitement not fear. As the crowd approached so it grew. Middle aged women joined it. Men joined in. I have no doubt that if there had been elephants and geese and hippotamuses in the Avenue de l'Opera they too would have joined in the tidal wave of enthusiasm. We stood and waited for there was nowhere to go and nothing to do but wait for the onslaught to reach us.

But the mob ran past us. They didn't stop. They didn't produce autograph books or record albums for Elvis to sign. They just ran on. I suppose there were no more than two or three hundred of them but they were a frightening sight. Out of curiosity we hurried after them, curious to see what magnetic force was drawing them forward.

We stopped, eventually, at the back of a sizeable crowd. We could hear screaming, plenty of screaming, but we could see nothing. It must have been a strange feeling for Elvis, to be at the back of such a crowd, instead of at the front, the centre of its attention.

'What is it all about?' I asked a man of about 35. He was the only person around us who wasn't waving or jumping or shouting or screaming. His female companion was almost beside herself with excitement.

He looked at me as though I'd just arrived from Mars. 'Johnny.'
'Johnny Hallyday?'
'Bien sur!' he replied. Of course. 'Ce que les autres Johnny est-il?' What other Johnny is there? 'Il est le Elvis Presley francais'. He is the French Elvis Presley.

We should not have been surprised. There was, at the time, no greater star in France. And his star was still high in the sky over 30 years later. Few American or British stars enjoy such longevity. It seemed that Johnny had come out of the hotel and had climbed into a motor car. He had smiled and waved. It was enough. How do crowds of people know when these major events are taking place? I do not know. Elvis, whom you might imagine would have known, did not know then and does not know now. Crowds of fans behave like birds migrating, following some strange hidden forces, influenced by powerful compulsions they probably cannot perceive with their senses but which are there nevertheless.

    We wandered away. I told Elvis what the man had said. Elvis smiled at me. The irony of the situation was not wasted on us. We wandered north, into the lower reaches of the 18th arrondissement, towards Montmartre and Sacre Coeur. In the daytime this is a busy working class area which caters for the thousands of tourists who want to photograph the timeless beauties of Montmartre and wander along streets used by Renoir and Toulouse-Lautrec. At night the area becomes the home of the Moulin Rouge, the can-can and a seemingly endless variety of ladies of the night who wander the streets dressed only in their underwear. We stopped to take refreshment in cafés which took our fancy. There is never any shortage of cafés in Paris. Go up the Eiffel Tower and you will find a café. There are probably cafés in the catacombs and the sewers.

    And, everywhere in Paris, despite the cold, we stood around in many parks watching Frenchmen play boules, also known as petanque. The French love this game. It is the game of and for the people. Walk through a park of any size, in any season and at almost any time of day and you will probably find a game in progress. The vast majority of players are male and are aged somewhere between 30 and 100. They seem to wear a standard uniform consisting of a blue or grey anorak and a pair of faded blue jeans. Every player has two steel boules, each boule being about the size of a cricket ball but much heavier, and the game bears a vague resemblance to bowls in that each player aims to get his balls as close as possible to the jack, a small wooden sphere slightly smaller than a table tennis ball. Since the game is played on fairly rough ground the balls are thrown rather than bowled.

    The game suits the French very well in that it involves virtually no physical exercise at all (players even use magnets on lengths of string so that they can pick up their boules without having to bend down) and absolutely no stress. We watched hundreds of boules matches but never once saw a player become agitated or distressed. Players usually carry a piece of string so that they can measure the distance between boules and the jack if there is any possible uncertainty about who has won a particular game. At the end of a session everyone shakes hands with everyone else and then goes home. No boules player bothers to keep score and so there are no disputes and there is no boasting. Boules is the sporting equivalent of sand sculpture in that it is a pleasure for the moment. Boules players are unique among Frenchmen in that they never kiss one another on the cheeks.

The original version of the game allowed players to take a run up of one or two paces before letting go of their steel boule. This is now known as the 'jeu provencale' version of the game. The rules were changed in Marseilles to accommodate a player called Jules Le Noir who was confined to a wheelchair as a result of an accident. In order that their friend could continue to play, the men with whom he regularly played changed the rules so that players had to stand or sit when throwing their boule. Run ups were banned. The game was described as 'pieds tanques' (feet together) and so the game of 'petanque' was born. I have no doubt that removing this element of exercise was much to the delight of other players around the country for today 'jeu provencale' is played only rarely.

As we walked, we looked for a street or an area where we would like to live. Ideally, we wanted somewhere quiet and within walking distance of Notre Dame, the Opera, the Champs Élysées and the Eiffel Tower. We also wanted to live in an area where there were a couple of decent supermarkets, at least one good bakery and a variety of other essential shops such as a pharmacy and a newsagent. There are some areas of Paris that look pleasant enough but which turn out either to contain nothing but offices or shops selling souvenir T-shirts, berets, key rings and postcards to tourists. We wanted to live in an area of Paris that seemed more like a village than a corner of a huge theme park.

Chapter Thirty Five

It was at about this time that Elvis discovered that there were almost as many Elvis Presley lookalike competitions in Paris as there had been in America. He'd been looking at photographs he'd developed, taken inside a club in Montparnasse, when he noticed, stuck on a wall, a poster advertising an Elvis contest. And it wasn't long before the inevitable happened.

'What the hell were you thinking of?' I demanded, when I heard that he'd paid a 20 franc entrance fee so that he could take part in a competition to find out whether or not he was any good at impersonating himself.

'It'll be fun,' he grinned. 'There's a 500 franc prize for the winner!'

'The minute you open your mouth they'll realise that you're the real Elvis!'

Elvis shook his head. 'Have you heard some of these guys? I heard a couple of the other contestants rehearsing. They sound more like me than I ever did. One of them could even do the lip thing.'

I looked at him, couldn't think of anything to say, and just hung my head. It seemed to me to be an absurd and unnecessary risk. I was convinced that this was going to be the end. What laws had we broken? Would we be extradited? How serious is it to pretend to be dead? What are the penalties for helping someone to pretend to be dead? I couldn't get my head around the possible consequences. But I have to confess that, at the same time that I was worried sick, I was also intrigued to find out what happened. Who wouldn't have been?

That first contest was held on a Saturday night and the club was packed. A good many of the patrons, there just to watch the contest rather than to perform, were dressed as Elvis. I even spotted a couple of girls who had combed their hair into Elvis style quiffs and had combed down chunks of hair to give themselves fairly convincing false sideburns.

There were twelve contestants and the standard was higher than I'd expected. Most of the fake singers were chubby bordering on obese and were obviously imitating the later version of Elvis. Four were quite slim and were clearly impersonating the original. There was a judging panel of three – two men and a woman. One of the men was the owner of the club and the other was a music critic I'd seen around. The woman was a young jazz club singer who I knew earned most of her living performing backing vocals on pop records. I'd even heard a rumour that she had performed the lead vocals on bestselling records made by teenage stars who couldn't sing as well as they looked. She had a large nose, large ears, wide-set eyes, eyebrows that looked like hairy caterpillars, a flat chest and almost no chance of making it as a singer herself.

Elvis, who had promised that he wouldn't try too hard, reneged and did his best to act and sound like his old self. He was the third contestant and performed 'Love Me Tender' and 'Don't Be Cruel'. He accompanied himself on the guitar he'd bought from the Depot Vente store. 'I was going to forget the words and croak a bit,' he told me. 'But the competition was too good. I'd have come last if I hadn't made a bit of an effort.' A bit of an effort! He did the hip thing three times and if his upper lip had curled any more it would have rolled up his nose. Because of the haircut he wore an Elvis wig which he'd bought from a shop which specialised in party costumes. Not surprisingly it looked like a cheap wig, the sort people wear at parties. Several members of the audience were wearing exactly the same model.

Despite all his efforts Elvis came seventh.

'Number three was too stiff and too earnest,' said the club owner, giving his judgement.

'There wasn't enough movement of the hips,' complained the female singer. The winner, whom she praised to the skies, had spent his entire set wiggling his hips as though trying to keep a hula hoop off the floor. She afterwards made a point of confronting Elvis and telling him that she thought he didn't deserve to come as high as seventh. 'You were one of the worst,' she told him. 'Superficially, you look a little bit like Elvis but you really didn't manage to capture the essence of the man. And your voice was very unconvincing. You don't have a good voice and your vocal range is quite different to Elvis's.'

The music critic complained that Elvis was neither as thin as the original Elvis nor as fat as the later version. 'A pleasant enough amateur attempt,' he said, rather patronisingly, 'but not really good enough for a public performance.'

Of the five contestants beaten by Elvis, three were teenagers who did not seem to me to have ever seen Elvis perform, and two were men in their sixties who sweated a good deal and had both disguised their bald patches with comb over hair styles. One of them accompanied himself by banging on a tambourine a la Mick Jagger. All five over-exaggerated Elvis's mannerisms in the way that amateur impersonators invariably do.

Elvis regularly entered other similar competitions but I never worried about them in the way that I had worried about that first contest. The best he ever did was come fifth and on that occasion there were only five contestants. He won a free drink at the bar and a packet of something that looked like pork scratchings. Elvis eventually accepted that he would be unlikely to do better than this, acknowledging that successful impersonators always exaggerate the mannerisms and characteristics of the people they are imitating and so, to a certain extent, they become more like the original than the original himself.

'I should have won,' said Elvis, rather sadly, on that occasion.

I looked at him and raised an eyebrow. 'Of course you should have bloody well won!'

He looked back at me and then grinned and did the lip thing.

Chapter Thirty Six

Our efforts in the night clubs, jazz clubs and theatres of Paris helped increase the circulation of *The American in Paris* by a tiny amount but Hildy told us miserably that the improvement in our circulation had been measured in hundreds, rather than the thousands he said we needed to keep the newspaper alive. It was the usual publishing story. A low circulation meant not only that the print cost per copy of the paper was high but also that businesses in Paris were unwilling to buy advertising space. Hildy believed that the future of the paper depended upon our printing a real scoop; a news story that the other papers in Paris didn't have. He seemed to have forgotten that he was publishing and editing a weekly paper which appealed to its readers because it contained snippets of gossip that other papers didn't bother to report.

And then it appeared as though the paper had an unexpected slice of amazing luck.

Elvis and I climbed the stairs to the top floor at about nine thirty one Wednesday morning to be confronted by an editor with a broad grin. This was something of a first. Neither of us had ever even seen Hildy looking quite as cheerful.

'I've got a scoop!' our employer announced, looking as pleased with himself as any cat with a well-fed canary firmly in its claws. The smile which had greeted us then suddenly disappeared; switched off to avoid waste. It was as though smiles cost money and had to be carefully rationed.

We stared at him in astonishment. Ours was not a newspaper which attracted scoops. Where would we get them? When one of the city's many freelance reporters and stringers picked up a good story they would either telephone one of the big French papers or the Paris desk of one of the American or British publications. Why would they bother to ring us when we didn't have any money to pay for story tips? Our best pages were filled with gossip gleaned from hotel doormen, café owners and club bouncers. We paid them with free copies of the paper, an occasional drink and free plugs for the establishment where they worked. Hildy filled the rest of our pages with second hand news taken from the 'proper' newspapers. News stories concerning earthquakes, wars, political misbehaviour and economic disasters were taken, having been carefully rewritten, from the 'New York Times', 'Le Figaro', 'The Daily Telegraph', 'The Washington Post', 'Le Monde' and 'Liberation'. Our sports stories came from 'l'Equipe'. If there was a summit meeting in Paris Hildy would take our coverage, such as it was, from Parisian newspapers such as 'Le Parisien'. Our spiciest bits and pieces of news and national gossip were pulled from weekly periodicals such as the French satirical publications, 'Charlie Hebdo' and 'Le Canard Enchaine'; the colourful 'Paris-Match' and 'Le Point' and 'L'Express'. Hildy's newspaper bill would have been astronomical if it had not been for the fact that French newspaper and magazine proprietors provided one another with complimentary copies of their publications. In return we used to send them all a free copy of *The American In Paris*. There isn't much doubt that we had the best of this particular deal.

'What sort of scoop?' asked Elvis. 'What's the story?'

'A lovely, juicy murder!' said Hildy, his eyes gleaming. 'Have you heard about the man who was killed in an alley near St Julien le Pauvre?'

'The church opposite Notre Dame?' I asked. 'The one near Shakespeare and Company?'

'That's the one.'

Elvis and I had visited the church just a couple of weeks earlier. It's an amazing piece of architecture. The building took 300 years to build and generation after generation of carpenters and stone masons worked on it, keeping the work in the family throughout.

I looked at Elvis. He looked back at me and shook his head. Neither of us had heard of any murder near St Julien.

'This is really a scoop? No one else has the story?'

Hildy looked at his watch. 'The news agencies will have it now,' he admitted. 'And the story will be on the radio and television in a few minutes time. Tomorrow morning's papers will have the news I suppose. But we'll also be on the streets tomorrow morning. We can have this story as quickly as anyone else. It's a genuine, Paris news story.' He paused and sighed contentedly. He then smiled broadly. This smile was even broader than the smile which had greeted us. It lasted a few moments longer, too. It was the first time I'd realised just how different two smiles can be. Whenever Elvis smiled I felt as though the sun had come out. He smiled with his whole face. His eyes sparkled. Most film stars have stunning smiles and all big stars can turn on their very best smile at whim. Elvis could. But Hildy's smile was, quite simply, terrifying. It reminded me of Christopher Lee's vampire smile. His lips went up at the corners. But that was all. His eyes remained as cold as ice and as empty as a worked out mine. This was, I realised, only the second time I'd seen it. It occurred to me that I wouldn't worry if I never saw it again.

Hildy believed that the timing of this story was so fortunate for us that it was our lucky break. Our newspaper went to the printers at three o'clock on Wednesday afternoons. If we missed that deadline the paper wouldn't be printed, and wouldn't be ready for distribution to our customers, ready to be sold on the following morning. The timing could not have been better. If the murder had been committed on a Thursday we would have had to wait a week to report it and by then, of course, the news would have been too old to be of any interest. And, if Hildy had received his tip a few hours later, we wouldn't have been able to use it for another week – unless we'd produced an extra edition, something which would have been horrifyingly expensive and, therefore, quite out of the question.

'How did you get the story?' I asked.

Hildy shook his head and the smile disappeared. It was like a light being switched off. One minute the smile was there. The next minute it had gone. No magician ever got rid of a rabbit as quickly as Hildy got rid of that damned smile. 'Can't tell you that,' he said, clutching and savouring his secret as though it were a lover. 'But we're running the story on pages one, two and three. I want you two to get down there now. Take some pictures and get some background colour.'

'What sort of pictures do you want?' asked Elvis.

'Whatever you can get,' replied Hildy. 'A picture of the church, a few snaps of the police milling around, even a picture of that tape that they put round a crime scene, pictures of people standing around watching what's going on. Anything you can get.'

'And what do you need from me?' I asked.

'General background,' said Hildy. 'Who was killed, what he was doing there, why he was killed, who found the body, if the police think it's an isolated killing or if they suspect that a serial killer is starting his career, any clues the police will give you, any ideas they have about the murderer.' He looked at the clock. 'Be back here by one o'clock so we can put the story to bed in time for you to get everything over to the printers in time.' Back in the 1970's, of course, there were no mobile telephones and no internet. Hildy knew as well as I did that the few telephones down near the crime scene would be permanently occupied by junior reporters working for the big papers. They would occupy the phones and keep the lines open so that when more senior reporters appeared with their latest piece of news they could get straight through to the news room. And the same thing would be happening in nearby cafés and bars.

Elvis and I didn't waste any time trying to gouge more information out of Hildy. Infected by his enthusiasm we raced downstairs, found a taxi and told the driver to hurry to the crime scene. This always works in films but never works for me in real life. 'Je ne vais pas briser la limite de vitesse,' said the driver haughtily. I will not break the speed limit. He deliberately positioned himself behind an elderly Peugeot being driven by a little old lady who was so small that she had to look between the spokes of the wheel to drive her car. I closed my eyes, took a big breath and counted to ten. This was Elvis's first big news story. As we sat in the back of the taxi I looked at him. He had a broad grin on his face. He was enjoying himself.

'Got plenty of film?' I asked.

He tapped his camera bag. 'Twelve rolls, each one with 36 exposures,' he said. He suddenly looked worried. 'Do you think that will be enough?'

'I think so,' I told him with a smile. 'Twelve rolls will give you just over 400 pictures; that should be enough.' I leant forward in the cab and offered the taxi driver 100 francs to go faster. 'Allez vous nourrir ma famile et acheter des chaussures pour mes enfants si je perds mon permis?' he demanded. 'Will you feed my family and buy shoes for my children if I lose my licence?'

I put the note back into my wallet, sat back and closed my eyes. Elvis put a hand on my arm. 'Relax,' he said. 'The police will still be there in ten hours time.' He grinned at me. 'No one's going to be interested in this story anyway. We'd be better off making up stuff about Cary Grant's visit to the Crazy Horse night club last night.'

'Was Cary Grant in the Crazy Horse?' I asked him.

Elvis smiled and shrugged. 'I've no idea,' he said. 'But the readers would much rather buy a paper with the headline 'Was Cary Grant In Crazy Horse Night Club?' than buy one with the headline 'Unidentified Tramp Murdered Near River.''

We were back in the Rue Bonarparte with a couple of hours to spare before the newspaper had to be put to bed at the printers. Elvis disappeared into the tiny dark room which Hildy had installed and fitted out so that his photographers wouldn't have to waste time (or money) having their film developed by commercial photo shops.

'Write what you've got,' Hildy told me. 'No more than 800 words.'

I sat down in front of the typewriter I used in the newspaper's offices. It was an old Remington which was so primitive that it had probably been used by Mark Twain and it generally sat on a corner of a desk in a dark corner of Hildy's office. To use the typewriter I always had to clear away piles of newspapers, press releases, photographic prints and unopened letters. I had to bang the keys really hard to force them to leave ink marks on the paper and after a few minutes my fingers were always sore and sometimes bleeding.

In my article I described how two drunks heading home at four in the morning had found an old tramp lying in a pool of blood in an alleyway behind St Julien's church. His head had been bashed in by the traditional blunt object, which had never been found and which the police rather suspected might have been tossed into the conveniently situated river Seine. The detective I spoke to didn't seem terribly interested in the crime. There are many tramps in Paris and this one had no identification in his pockets. While Elvis took pictures of nothing very much a waiter I vaguely recognised wandered over to where I was standing. He worked at a café just around the corner. 'I rang your paper with the news about this,' he told me. 'I thought you might pay me for the tip off.' When I asked him why he hadn't rung one of the bigger newspapers he confessed that since his café sold our paper ours was the only telephone number he could find in a hurry. I offered him three 10 franc notes and when he looked disgusted I gave him two more. The tip wasn't worth that much and I felt a fool handing over the money.

'The murderer was almost certainly another tramp,' a policeman had told me. 'The body was found near to a doorway and the two were probably fighting over who had the right to sleep there. Or they may have been fighting over a bottle of cheap wine.' Life and death have always been cheap among the clochards of Paris. The sad murder of an anonymous tramp wasn't the sort of story we usually reported and although it may sound cruel and rather heartless I couldn't really see that our readers would be terribly excited to read about the death of an unknown vagrant.

And in the end, my fears were justified. We sold far fewer copies of that edition than of our usual editions. It seemed clear that the readers found our made up news stories far more enticing than real news stories. It was another one of life's small lessons. It hit Hildy really hard. He had, it seemed, genuinely believed that he was, for once, about to break a big story. He had always thought of himself as a real newspaperman; an old-fashioned journalist, the sort who wore a green eyeshade, shouted `Copy!' and smelt of ink. But there was sometimes a naivety about him. Elvis and I suspected that Hildy had grabbed at the story for no other reason than that it had arrived at a well-timed moment.

The really funny thing was that although he had no experience as a newspaperman even Elvis instinctively knew that the murder scoop wouldn't prove popular with the readers. He knew what people really wanted to read. `People who buy newspapers and magazines don't much care whether or not the stories are real,' he told me immediately afterwards. `People just want to read interesting stuff, and they will always prefer something that is made up and interesting to something that is true and boring.

`That's why people refer to newspaper articles as `stories'!' I told him.

Chapter Thirty Seven

On the day after our big 'scoop', Elvis and I eventually decided that we would take two adjacent flats in an apartment building close to the Rue de Bellechasse; a quiet street in the 7th arrondissement on the left bank of the River Seine. (The left bank is the side of Paris which lies underneath the river when you look at the city on a street map. The right bank, I'm pleased to say, is the part of the city which lies on the other side of the river.) At its end furthest from the river the Rue de Bellechasse (literally the street of good hunting) runs alongside and between a number of huge ministry buildings which are, of course, deserted at night, at weekends and on public holidays. We decided that even in the daytime, during working hours, there wouldn't be much noise coming from them. Civil servants don't do a lot of singing and dancing and the production of red tape is a pretty quiet affair. Moreover, since the Ministere des Armees was just around the corner there were plenty of police and army patrols in the area and so it seemed likely that burglars and hoodlums would probably choose some other area to ply their trades. At its river end the Rue de Bellechasse ran between the Gare d'Orsay and the Chancellerie for the Legion d'Honneur. When we moved into our flats the Gare d'Orsay was still a disused railway station. It wouldn't become an art museum for nearly another decade. We both decided that it would be difficult, if not impossible, to find a quieter and better protected street in central Paris. Our building had the added advantage of having a separate exit which took us through a small courtyard and a narrow alleyway into one of the neighbouring streets. There had been no signs that our secret would ever be exposed but it was comforting to know that if necessary we had an excellent escape route.

   The flats were almost identical in the way they were laid out. Both had a living room, a dining room, two bedrooms, a decent sized kitchen, a bathroom and a separate WC. There were no views of the Eiffel Tower or Sacre Coeur (in films every window in every flat seems to have a view of one or both of these landmarks) but we were within strolling distance of good shops, cinemas and great cafés. We each also had a small cave or cellar room in the basement of the building and a tiny chambre de bonne or maid's room in the attic. We knew that the cellars would be useful for storing the junk we didn't yet have but would inevitably accumulate over the years. Elvis decided that he would turn his attic room into a darkroom and I decided that I would turn mine into a writing room. Apart from the tiny attic rooms above us our apartments were on the top floor, which we both felt was a huge advantage because it meant that we didn't have to worry about heavy footed neighbours practising the rumba. The building had a tiny but rather quaint ascenseur or lift fitted with those delightful, old-fashioned metal folding gates. The woman from the property company was proud of the lift but at the time neither Elvis nor I were too bothered by its presence. We were young enough, and fit enough, to be able to get upstairs faster by using the stairs. Today, we are very grateful for its presence because it means that we don't have to carry our shopping up five flights of stairs though the lift, which has been renovated at least three times over the years, is so small that if two people travel in it together there is hardly room to carry any shopping.

    Both flats were for sale but the owner, a small French property company run by brothers from Marseilles, was also willing to rent them out and to give us an option to buy if we liked them. We decided that we would rent for a year and then, if we were both happy there, Elvis would buy the two apartments and I would pay rent to him rather than to the property company. For reasons which will become clear things didn't quite work out as we had planned but today we still live in those same apartments and neither of us has any plans to move. I think it is fair to say that when we leave we won't be going to live anywhere else. We have both managed to fill our cellars with junk. Elvis still has his darkroom in the attic, though he's removed the blackout blinds now that he uses a digital camera. My attic room still contains a writing desk and a few shelves of reference books, though today the desk contains a laptop instead of a typewriter. This book is being written there.

Chapter Thirty Eight

Hildy's disappointment over the scoop that didn't sell copies of the paper broke his heart. He'd wanted *The American in Paris* to be a proper newspaper, a real competitor to the 'International Herald Tribune' and he had genuinely believed that a news story describing the murder of a tramp would give the paper the gravitas he craved. It turned out later that his real name wasn't Hildy at all. He'd borrowed the name from the character Hildy Johnson played by Jack Lemon in the 1974 film 'The Front Page', by Rosalind Russell in the 1940 version (called His Girl Friday) and by Pat O'Brien in the 1931 original. The realisation that the readers didn't share his dream was too much for him to bear. When Elvis and I arrived at the offices the following Tuesday we found him lying slumped on his desk. He hadn't eaten himself to death, died of a surfeit of cheap red wine or died of a literally broken heart; he'd died because he'd put a .38 revolver into his mouth, aimed upwards and pulled the trigger.

We didn't touch anything, but telephoned the police. There didn't seem much point in calling an ambulance because there wasn't anything doctors could do for him. The police took one look at Hildy's corpse, asked us a few questions, made a few notes and then they called an ambulance to come and take the body away. Even though a six-year-old child could have spotted the cause of death the authorities always like to have these things done properly; post mortem, a doctor's written report and a lot of paperwork.

The ambulance men tried for an hour to squeeze Hildy's body through the door before admitting defeat. They had to move him down to street level by poking him through a window onto one of the multi-storey lifts that furniture removers use to get beds, sofas, fridges and cookers in and out of Parisian apartments. They park the lift in the street, send the platform up to the desired floor and move the furniture in or out of the window. Hildy was too fat even to go through the window and the removal men had to take out the frame before they could get him through. It was the sort of story our readers would have loved. At one point it had seriously looked as though we were going to have to call in an embalmer, have Hildy preserved and then stuffed in a cupboard for long-term storage. One of the workmen who was called in to take out the window frame suggested that we might consider soaking Hildy in formalin, standing him up in a corner, calling in a bricklayer and preserving him within the fabric of the building. Elvis and I agreed that Hildy would have liked that but the policemen, who had stayed with us to make sure that everything was done properly, wouldn't hear of it.

Elvis and I didn't know what to do with the newspaper when Hildy had gone but we felt instinctively that Hildy would have wanted us to make sure that we got the next edition out on time. He hadn't been an easy person to like, and almost impossible to get to know, but he'd given us work when we needed it and our days working for *The American in Paris* had been great fun. We put out the next week's issue and were proud that we hit the deadline. *The American in Paris* was on the city's streets, bar counters and reception desks precisely on time. I remember we spent several hours sitting in a café trying to think up good headlines for the front page of that remembrance issue. Elvis suggested the headline 'Is Elvis Presley Alive And Living In Paris?' but although it made me smile I vetoed the proposal on the grounds that it wasn't a terribly good idea to put the notion into people's heads. Instead we filled the front page with a picture of Jim Morrison's grave and the headline: 'Is Jim Morrison Alive And Living In Paris?' Our story spread around the world and it still appears in newspapers and magazines occasionally. We filled the rest of the paper with the sort of lightweight stuff the readers seemed to like and gave Hildy a good send off on page three. It was his paper, after all. He'd founded it, published it, built it up and edited it and he still owned it. We didn't have the foggiest idea whether or not he had any relatives or had left a will. For all we knew the paper might now be owned by a dogs' home in Pennsylvania. We didn't know much about him or his life, and nor did anyone else he knew, but together Elvis and I managed to cobble together an obituary that I think he would have liked. We described him as a former C.I.A. agent who had run an underground newspaper in Paris during World War II and who had been a secret advisor to three unnamed American Presidents. We described him as one of America's foremost journalists and editors and a man who had lectured at both Harvard and Yale. He had, we wrote, been a member of the American team at three consecutive (but unspecified) Winter Olympics and had left his extensive collection of paintings and sculptures to the Louvre Museum. We explained the absence of any family by reporting that Hildy had for many years been the secret lover of Hollywood legend Tallulah Bankhead whose tragic and early death in 1968 had left him heartbroken. It was a pretty impressive obituary and Elvis and I were proud of it. We were certain Hildy would have been pleased with it too. The two things Hildy had taught us were first, that if you wanted to make stuff up you had to be sure that you did not build your story upon an unstable foundation and second, that it should be be damned near impossible for anyone to disprove anything you write. We weren't likely to have any trouble with the C.I.A. because they never admit or deny that any individual is linked to the organisation. We knew that it would be enormously difficult to prove who had or had not lectured at Harvard and Yale universities and who could say who has or has not been a secret advisor to a President? We hadn't defined Hildy's contribution to the American Winter Olympic team and the late Ms Bankhead's reputation wasn't likely to be damaged by the addition of another lover to her fine collection.

We would have undoubtedly dealt with his obituary rather differently if we'd known that there were any relatives around but no one we spoke to had ever heard our publisher talk about wives, children, parents or siblings. Hildy had a notaire who worked in scruffy offices in the 5th arrondissement and who, according to papers we'd found in a drawer, had been responsible for drawing up Hildy's rental agreement with his landlord. The notaire had been the first person we'd visited. He told us firmly that as far as he was aware Hildy was totally alone in the world. There were no relatives. And there was no will. He said that he would put notices in official French and American publications in the slight hope that a relative might come forward. But he pointed out that Hildy owned no property (the warren of tiny top floor rooms where he lived and published the newspaper were rented) and said that his only asset was *The American in Paris*. We all agreed that since the newspaper only just about broke even it wasn't likely to prove enormously attractive to Rupert Murdoch, Robert Maxwell, Jimmy Goldsmith or Kerry Packer.

And then, while clearing out a filing cabinet in the newspaper offices, I found a letter dated March 1969 telling someone called Eugene that his sister Poppy had died. The letter had been written by Poppy's daughter, a young woman called Carol Harding, and had been forwarded from another address in Paris. I assumed that Eugene was probably Hildy and that Poppy's daughter must be Hildy's niece. It was clear from the letter that the young woman had never met Eugene, and didn't know that he now called himself Hildy. It was also clear from the letter that Hildy and his sister had not been in touch for a long, long time. I got the impression that this was not a close knit family. There was no sign that Hildy had replied to the letter, no carbon copy of a response and no scribbled note on Poppy's letter recording that an acknowledgement had been sent. But the letter from Poppy's daughter did include a telephone number and an address in London where Carol had been living at the time of her mother's death.

Since it was the only clue we had I rang the number, not expecting to speak to anyone who knew what I was talking about. To my great surprise, I found myself speaking to Carol herself.

'I'm afraid I have some bad news,' I told her. 'Your Uncle Hildy has passed away.'

'My Uncle Who?'

'Hildy.'

'I don't have an Uncle Hildy.'

'I have a letter here from you telling him about the death of his sister, your mother Poppy.'

There was an unpleasant sounding snort at the other end of the telephone. 'I had an Uncle Eugene.'

'Yes, sorry, that would be him. I knew him as Hildy.'

'Who are you?'

I told her my name, the one I was using, and explained that I had worked on Hildy's newspaper.

'He has a newspaper?'

'Yes. A weekly paper here in Paris.'

'He owned it?'

'Yes.'

'Was he rich?'

'Not really, I'm afraid. There doesn't seem to be any money and he didn't own any property and the newspaper has quite a small circulation.'

She sounded disappointed but asked me for the newspaper's address. I told her, explaining that it was also where Hildy lived.

'He lived in the offices?'

'Yes. It was a very small newspaper. There isn't much money I'm afraid. At least I don't think there is.'

'I'll come over,' she said. 'On the boat and the train. Did he have a lawyer?'

'Yes. He had a notaire.'

'What's a notaire?'

'He's a lawyer who works for the Government and deals with legal documents such as contracts and wills.'

'That's a good sign. If there was a lawyer then there must have been some money. I hope there's enough to make it worth my while.'

'Do you know if Hildy, sorry Eugene, had any other relatives? A widow? Children perhaps?'

Carol laughed, rather unpleasantly I thought. 'There was no widow, no wife and, as far as I know, no children. I'm all he had and the last time I saw him I was seven-years-old. He thought I was a boy and bought me a gun that fired caps as a birthday present.'

She said she'd catch the train the following day. I got the impression she didn't have anything to keep her in London.

'Do you want us to keep publishing the paper?' I asked her.

'Us? Did my Uncle Eugene have staff? How many of you damned people are there? Are you still being paid? I hope you're not stealing from the estate.'

I bit my tongue, tried to convince myself that the poor woman was shocked at the news to hear of the death of her much loved uncle, was grieving at his loss and was clearly not herself. I patiently explained that Elvis and I had worked with her Uncle Eugene, that we weren't officially employed by him, that we weren't being paid and that even if we were that way inclined there wasn't anything in the office to steal unless she counted unsold and unsaleable copies of the paper, a couple of ancient typewriters that had been probably been thrown out by Mark Twain, a drowsy cat and a few paperclips. She said she'd see us sometime in the evening on the following day and that we might as well prepare the next edition of the paper for publication but that she would make a decision about the paper's future when she met us.

Chapter Thirty Nine

Elvis and I awaited the arrival of Hildy's niece with some trepidation. We couldn't get used to thinking of him as Eugene. He wasn't a Eugene. He was a Hildy through and through. And if he wanted to call himself Hildy then that was fine with us. We were, after all, both using names which weren't the ones we were born with.

'Is this it?' she demanded, when she had got her breath back. Those who argue that obesity is the result of an inherited gene would have been delighted to see what Hildy's niece was built along the same substantial lines as the Great Man himself. She just about managed to squeeze in through the door.

Elvis and I introduced ourselves and then confirmed that what she could see was, indeed, 'it'.

'Where are the printing presses?' she demanded.

I explained that the newspaper was actually printed at another site, by a printing company. She didn't seem terribly pleased to hear this. She looked around, still wheezing, and picked up an old copy of the paper. We had carefully hidden the copies of the edition which contained Hildy's slightly imaginative obituary.

'Is this it? *The American in Paris.*'

We agreed that she was, indeed, holding a copy of *The American in Paris*.

She flicked through it. 'People buy this rubbish?'

'A few do,' Elvis confirmed. He gave her the smile. She didn't even notice.

'How many?'

Elvis and I looked at each other.

'How many copies do you sell?'

'A couple of thousand. Sometimes three thousand. We once sold three and a half thousand.'

'Three and a half thousand copies? In a week?'

'That was our biggest week,' I said. 'We had a picture of Jane Fonda on the front page.'

'Jane Fonda?'

'She's a film star. She used to be married to Roger Vadim.'

'I know who Jane Fonda is. Who the hell is Roger Vadim?'

'He's a French film director,' said Elvis. 'He and Fonda were married.'

'So why was she on the front page?'

'There was a rumour that she was in Paris.'

'Was she?'

'Was she what?'

'Was she in Paris.'

'I don't know. I'm not sure. Possibly.'

'She had a new film out and we were sent some good publicity stills,' I said. 'There was some talk that she would be here for the Premiere. And might meet Vadim.'

'Talk?'

'A porter at one of the hotels told us that he'd heard people talking in the lift.'

She looked at Elvis, and then at me. I had to admit that when you analysed it closely the story didn't seem all that substantial. 'Pathetic. And with that rubbish on the front page you still only managed to sell 3,500 copies?'

'It was quite a lot for us.'

'Has the paper ever made any money?'

'I don't think so. I think it made enough for Hildy to live on.'

'Eugene.'

'Eugene.'

'My Uncle Eugene had a small pension. It died when he died. He used to work for the U.S. Postal Service.'

'The Postal Service?'

'He was a retired postman. He delivered letters. He took early retirement because he had a glandular illness.'

'His weight made it difficult for him to get around?'

'He had a glandular illness.'

'Yes. Of course.'

'I assume the paper also made enough money to support the two of you?' She made it sound as though we'd been leeching off Uncle Eugene.

'Not really. He usually paid us in newspapers which we had to sell. Occasionally he gave us a few francs. It wasn't a very profitable enterprise. But I think it could be, given time.'

'I'm not prepared to give it time or to waste any more money on what seems to me to be an entirely self-indulgent exercise. I'll go and see the lawyer in the morning. But you can take it that you're both fired. You don't work here any longer. Do you have any keys I should have?'

I took the door key out of my trouser pocket and handed it to her.

She looked at Elvis. 'You?'

Elvis shook his head.

'You're closing the paper?' I asked.

'I'm closing it,' she confirmed. 'There isn't any point in keeping it going if it doesn't make any money. I rather assume that Uncle Eugene used his pension money to keep the thing going. Well, his pension has gone and the paper is going. Whose is the cat?'

'The cat was Hildy's,' replied Elvis.

'Uncle Eugene's.'

'Hildy's.'

'Do you want it?'

'The cat?'

'Of course, the cat. If you want it you can take it. If you don't want it I'll find a vet and have it put to sleep.'

Elvis picked up the cat and we left.

'Nice woman,' said Elvis, as we walked away from Hildy's building for the last time.

'Sweet natured,' I agreed.

'What's its name?' asked Elvis. 'The cat I mean.'

I thought for a moment. 'I don't know. I don't think I ever heard Hildy call it anything except 'cat'.'

'So let's call it Hildy.'

'Is it a boy?'

'I don't have the foggiest. Unless they're ginger I've never found it easy to tell the sex of a cat.'

'What's different about the ginger ones?'

'They're all male.'

'Are they really? So we don't know if Hildy is a boy or a girl.'

'Does it matter?'

`It probably does to him. But since he won't be going outside the flat it won't matter very much. And it certainly doesn't matter a damn to us.' Paris is full of cats but most of them are full-time house cats, spending all their time indoors. Parisian roads are pretty dangerous for pedestrians, and some drivers do occasionally slow down a fraction if there is a pedestrian on the road directly ahead of them. Cats receive no such favours.

We stopped off at a café and drank two cups of coffee each. The waiter brought a saucer of milk for the cat. We then took the cat back home. We hadn't yet moved into our new twin apartments. The cat settled down very quickly and lived with us for another eight years. We never knew where it had originally come from, how old it was or what its name had been. I'm delighted to say that we never saw Hildy's niece again. I saw Hildy's notaire a few months later and he told me that she had sold Hildy's furniture to a house clearance specialist. He said he thought that after the funeral expenses she might possibly have made just enough money to pay for her trip across the Channel and the couple of nights she spent in a small hotel if Hildy hadn't owed nearly five month's rent on his apartment. She was, apparently, furious when she found out that her trip had left her out of pocket. She had threatened to sue the notaire, Hildy's landlord, Elvis and me and, quite possibly, Hildy's cat.

Chapter Forty

We were now jobless again. This didn't matter for Elvis, who still had some cash left and had those valuable diamonds hidden in the ice tray, but it was important to me. I needed a job in order to eat and drink. I was determined not to live off Elvis's money.

But first we had to move into our new apartments. There wasn't enough stuff to require a professional removal company. All the furniture in the apartment we were leaving was rented. We'd visited La Samaritaine, the huge department store situated at the right bank end of the Pont Neuf, and ordered beds, chairs, tables and kitchen equipment for the new apartments. The store's staff had already delivered everything we'd purchased. The few clothes, books, records and music tapes which we had accumulated fitted easily into our suitcases. We carried them round to our new apartments in a couple of taxi rides. As we walked around our old apartment for the final time, I opened the refrigerator and took out the diamonds, still stored in the freezer compartment.

'We ought to turn these into cash,' I told Elvis. 'If you invest the proceeds you should be able to live very comfortably on the interest.'

'Great,' said Elvis. He had met a girl called Sophie two nights previously and he was far more interested in deciding where to take her that evening than he was in worrying about money. I'd lost count of the number of girlfriends he'd had since we'd arrived in Paris but so far none of them had lasted more than one or two nights. In America his girlfriends had mostly fitted a pattern but here in Paris his tastes had broadened. Most of the girls who had breakfasted with us had been in their late teens or early twenties, slim and girlish in appearance, but there had also been a very fair sprinkling of older, plumper bed-mates. I've never been very good at judging women's ages but I rather suspected that Sophie, for example, was a year or two older than Elvis. She was a divorcee, lived in an apartment in the suburbs and came into Paris to work in the soft furnishings department of La Samaritaine. Elvis had met her when buying bedroom furniture for his apartment. She had been passing through the bed department with an armful of cushions and, as anyone would, he had persuaded her to join him on a bed he was testing. 'I want to make sure there's room for two,' he'd told her, undoubtedly turning on the smile at full voltage He once confided in me that it had been a great joy to discover that women were ready to go to bed with him as a person rather than as a legend.

 I honestly believe that if I had forgotten about the diamonds he too would have forgotten all about them. The next resident in the flat would have had a pleasant and extremely profitable surprise when they wanted a couple of ice cubes to drop into a drink. For a man who had almost certainly been the highest earning show business performer in history he has always taken remarkably little interest in financial matters. I've heard of quite a few stars who know to a penny how much they're earning, what percentages they're paying to which managers and where their money is invested. When he'd been living at Graceland, Elvis had allowed the Colonel to deal with all financial matters. As long as there was money available to buy an endless series of Cadillacs, to give away to strangers, and to pay for an equally endless series of huge peanut and jelly sandwiches, he really hadn't wanted to know how much money was coming in or how much was going out. He had trusted the Colonel implicitly and that had been both the reason for his towering success and the reason for his professional downfall. Would have he been Elvis Presley, the biggest star on the planet, without the instinctive touch of the Colonel, the professional huckster and arch manipulator? The answer is that he would almost certainly have not been the big star he became. Would he have been able to edge slowly into a dignified retirement if the Colonel hadn't been 'looking after' the money? Of course he would. The Colonel, an addicted gambler, had helped himself to far more of Elvis's earnings than could be thought fair and reasonable, and he had done nothing to curb Elvis's absurd spending habits. He had always assumed that the good times would roll on for ever and that whenever there were big bills to be paid (such as his own gambling debts in Las Vegas) it would be easy enough to deal with them by putting his 'boy' to work.

 Towards the end of the Graceland years Elvis had, at long last, begun to understand that he had to keep working in order to maintain his extraordinarily profligate lifestyle. There should have been millions invested in shopping malls and apartment buildings, or simply tucked away in inflation proof T bonds. But, apart from Graceland itself, and a couple of other small properties, there was almost no cash and no investment income. Elvis didn't blame anyone for this, and he certainly didn't blame the Colonel. It was just the way it was.

And now, in Paris, he seemed happy to allow me to deal with all his financial matters. But I did insist that he came with me when I went to sell the diamonds. 'We'll be carrying a big chunk of cash,' I pointed out, explaining that diamond merchants invariably bought and sold stones in exchange for notes. At that time no one who dealt in diamonds used cheques or credit cards. 'You can be my bodyguard.' Elvis, who was proud of his martial arts skills, liked that idea.

I'd found the addresses of three diamond merchants and jewellers in Paris and my plan was to take the diamonds to all three addresses and to then take the best price we were offered. The main diamond wholesalers in the city were then all in the third arrondissement, mainly congregated around the rue du Temple and not far from the Archives Nationales.

The deal with the Colonel and Vernon Presley was that they would give Elvis diamonds worth two million dollars. I knew it was unlikely that we would receive exactly that in cash since the value of diamonds, like all other commodities, goes up and down according to the market. In addition, of course, both lots of jewellers involved, the ones from whom the Colonel had bought the diamonds and the ones to whom we sold them, would want to take their cut. I thought that at the very least we would end up with 1.8 million dollars. I suspected that we would have to wait a while to allow our chosen jeweller to find the necessary cash. But when we set off across the river I was confident that we could get the deal done within the day. I was hoping that we would be able to complete the whole deal before mid-afternoon so that we could then put the cash into the safe deposit box we had already rented at our bank. I didn't mind keeping two million dollars worth of diamonds in the refrigerator but keeping two million dollars in cash seemed rather scary.

It was one of those glorious days that seem to be a speciality in Paris. The sky was blue, the weather warm and the light seemed at the same time both brighter and softer than it ever does anywhere else.

The first jeweller we visited was a Hassidic Jew and looked and sounded as if he had come straight out of central casting. Bu then clichés are clichés because they occur commonly. He wore a black three piece suit with a white shirt and no tie, a black homburg hat which he never removed, and reading spectacles perched right at the tip of a generously proportioned nose. He had a tiny shop and workroom in the rue Pastourelle. When I showed him the diamonds, sitting in a small and fairly ordinary purse I'd bought for the purpose, he took us into a back room, indicated that we should sit down in a couple of scruffy chairs and carefully poured the diamonds out onto a piece of black cloth. He placed a loupe in his right eye, and examined the first diamond. He didn't say a word. He then put the diamond down to one side and picked up the next one. He worked his way through all the diamonds like this. Elvis and I never took our eyes off the diamonds.

When he'd finished he took the loupe out of his eye, skilfully scooped up all the diamonds and put them back into the purse. He then closed the clasp at the top of the purse and handed it back to me.

'Did you think these were real?' he asked.

We stared at him, looked down at the purse I was now holding and then looked at one another. I couldn't believe what he'd said. Even now, twenty five years later, I can still remember every detail of that moment. The diamond dealer's face. He had seen the same disappointment many times before. Not for a moment had he suspected that we were trying to trick him. He knew that we were the ones who had been tricked. The dusty floor. The shelves containing small wooden boxes. The cutting equipment. The old-fashioned safe in a corner of the room. The dim light bulb, without a shade, which hung from the ceiling. The Anglepoise work lamp on the desk.

'They're not real?' I said. I knew it was me speaking because I heard my voice. But I felt far, far away. It did not seem possible that the Colonel and Vernon would have cheated Elvis in such a crude and cruel way. They both knew we could never do anything about it, of course. They both knew Elvis could not go back and confront them. A thousand questions raced through my mind. Did Vernon know that his son was being cheated? What the hell were we going to do now?

The dealer was surprisingly kind and sympathetic. He told us that the diamonds were good fakes and that he would give us twenty thousand francs for them. A few thousand dollars. He showed us one of the stones under a magnifying glass and pointed out how the girdles of the diamonds were slick, and un-faceted. He explained that real diamonds always have internal flaws but that ours had none.

'Take out one of your diamonds,' he said.

I unfastened the clasp on the purse and took out a diamond.

'Blow on it.'

I blew on it.

'You see the fog stays on the stone. Now blow on this one.' He took a diamond out of his waistcoat pocket and held it up. I blew. The fog disappeared almost immediately. He put his own diamond, a genuine stone, back into his waistcoat pocket.

'Lend me your diamond again for a moment,' he said.

I handed him one of our diamonds.

He showed us how we could read newsprint through our diamond but not through his real one. He used an ultraviolet light to show us the difference between our fake and his diamond. He put our stone into a glass of water. It almost completely disappeared. He put his stone into the same glass. It remained clearly visible. He weighed the two diamonds on a small scale and showed us how a fake diamond weighs more than a real one of the same size.

'Of course, it could be that your diamonds are the real ones and mine is a fake,' he said. 'Go to another dealer. Go to as many dealers as you like. Come back and I will give you cash money for your fakes.'

'Can you suggest another dealer we could try?' asked Elvis.

The dealer shook his head. 'I might tell him what to say. Find your own dealers. We might all try to cheat you on the price but we would not all send you away if the diamonds were real.'

We had planned to visit three dealers. We visited five. They all told us exactly the same thing. None of the other four were as kind or as patient as the first jeweller. After several of the most miserable hours of my life we went back and accepted that first dealer's offer of 20,000 francs. I gave him the purse as well. When he had handed us the money he opened the purse, took out one of the diamonds and handed it to Elvis.

'A souvenir,' he said. 'And a reminder.' He looked at us over his spectacles and wagged a finger. ' Be careful whom you trust.'

It was a terribly serious moment but I half expected him to burst into the first line of 'Reviewing the Situation' from Lionel Bart's 'Oliver!'

Chapter Forty One

I was far more upset than Elvis was. I was devastated. He didn't even seem angry. I could not believe that the Colonel had cheated Elvis, the star who had made him richer than any cheap huckster had a right to be. I did not want to believe that Vernon knew about the fake diamonds. But, in my heart, I could believe it. Elvis was going out of their lives. They were looking forward to managing his estate. What did they care about the man who had made it all possible? He could hardly come back, tell the world his death had all been a terrible mistake, or some overblown practical joke, and demand a recount. I was beginning to come to terms with all this and then it occurred to me that Elvis might wonder if I had switched the real stones for fake ones. Elvis was my friend and he trusted me. I was filled with silent fury at the knowledge that I had been put into an impossible situation.

'The way I look at it is this,' said Elvis, putting his arm around my shoulders. 'We went in there with a few bits of glass and came out with 20,000 francs.' He laughed. 'Let's go and find a decent café and have a coffee.'

I don't really know why but there and then I had a strange feeling that Elvis had known all along that the diamonds were fake. I remembered that whenever I had said that it was perhaps a good idea to turn the diamonds into cash he had thought up some reason to delay things.

We were walking back down towards the river and I suddenly halted and asked him if he'd known all along that we were carrying around a few bits of glass.

He stopped walking, came back a few paces, looked at me for a long, long time and then nodded.

'You knew?'

He shrugged, raised an eyebrow and then titled his head first to one side and then to the other. 'I didn't actually know…'

'But you suspected?'

'Yeah,' he said quietly. 'I suspected.'

'But why?'

'Because it's what they would do,' explained Elvis. He looked at me and thought for a while. 'They never thought I knew,' he said. 'But both the Colonel and my daddy were always cheating me. They thought there was so much money that it didn't matter a damn what they took. It was like the stuff was raining down from heaven. To them I guess it didn't seem like earned money, not like proper money that you have to work hard to get, not like money they give you after you've been bending your back for ten hours digging ditches or the money you get after driving a lorry for a week until your arm aches from the gear changing and your eyes ache from the staring and your neck aches and your back aches. The money that was coming into Graceland wasn't that sort of money. I spent a few hours in a recording studio and made a record and for months, years, afterwards the money just poured in from all over the world. Royalties from here, there and everywhere. They didn't see it as mine so much as ours. They didn't really understand where it came from or why it came and they thought that since someone had opened the tap it would never be closed. They could never accept the idea that one day I might stop performing, stop doing those shows in Vegas, because they were frightened that they wouldn't know how to cope without the money continuing to pour in. They were addicted to the lifestyle more than I ever was. I liked the singing and the playing and the performing. But it had all got out of hand.'

'But they cheated you! When they knew you were going away and would need the money. At the very time in your life when you needed them to be just a little honest they betrayed you. You were giving them everything. Millions in royalties and still they had to cheat you.'

'They don't have much in the way of imaginations,' said Elvis sadly. 'They were probably frightened just a little bit. Going into the unknown. Would the rainstorm come to a halt? When they knew I was going away then I stopped being part of the team. I became an outsider. And they are both greedy men. It's a shame to have to say it, particularly about my own daddy, but they are and there's no arguing against that. You saw them on the TV at the funeral. They knew I wasn't really dead so you could say they weren't being unduly disrespectful but they surely looked disrespectful. They were making a buck here and a buck there wherever they could. They'd have chopped up that corpse and sold little weeny bits at $20 a time if they could have got away with it.' He laughed. 'They probably thought about it!' He grabbed my arm and started walking again. 'Let's find a café, forget the coffee and buy ourselves a bottle of champagne to celebrate!'

'Celeberate?'

'Why not? We're starting over. The past has all gone. That guy with the swivelly hips ain't no more! There ain't no legacy, no great fortune. We'll make it, you and me, we'll find something to do.' He was genuinely positive, full of hope. I almost felt that he was glad the diamonds had turned out to be fake. No, that's wrong. I knew he was glad that the diamonds had turned out to be fake. He seemed relieved; as though a remaining burden had been lifted from his shoulders. I couldn't help wondering if he knew just how much this was going to affect us.

We were walking down one of the narrow streets in the third arrondissement, the part of Paris known as the Marais. It is the area of the city where French noblemen used to live and it is full still of splendid palaces and mansions known as 'hotels'. A pavement artist had reproduced one of Vermeer's paintings in chalk. It was 'The Girl With A Pearl Earring' and unbelievingly, frighteningly good. The artist had managed to capture the exact skin tones that Vermeer had portrayed. But he'd done it with chalk on concrete paving slabs. Coloured limestone scratched onto rough concrete. We both stopped and looked at it. If the picture had been on a canvas it would have looked good hanging on any wall. But here it would be washed away by the first rain shower or scuffed into powder by night time revellers. Elvis took the 20,000 francs out of his pocket, looked at me, grinned, and then tossed the bundle of money into the man's cap, where it joined the few coins other passers-by had donated.

'It's over,' said Elvis. 'The past is gone. Now we move on.'

'No regrets? You don't miss it? All that money raining down?'

'No,' said Elvis. 'Being Elvis would have killed me.' We walked on a few paces. 'It was killing me,' he added softly.

We stopped at a café and ordered two coffees. We couldn't afford the bottle of champagne. But the coffee was damned good.

We sat in a comfortable silence for a while and contemplated our future. Now that we both needed jobs there was a good deal to think about. The diamonds had lain in our refrigerator for more than six months and although they had always been more or less worthless I had believed them to be valuable and so, in a strange way, they had been valuable. It had, undeniably, been comfortable to know that they were there: two million dollars in waiting.

'So, what shall we do?' asked Elvis eventually. It was clear that he wasn't talking about the next few minutes. He was staring at a plumpish young woman sitting by herself at a table on the other side of the café. She was wearing a green, sleeveless dress that she seemed to have bought a few dozen cream cakes ago. It fitted her very well; cosily clinging to very feminine curves. She looked to be in her mid-thirties.

I didn't answer for a while. I was still thinking. The woman had noticed Elvis's interest in her. She had twice looked at him and she seemed to be blushing slightly.

'I think I'll just go and see if that young lady would like a little company,' Elvis said. He stood, picked up his cup of coffee, and wandered lazily across the café. He bent down and whispered something. The woman looked up at him, smiled and moved her handbag from the chair beside her.

A previous patron had left a newspaper on an adjoining table. I reached across and picked it up.

Chapter Forty Two

We weren't broke. That was the good news. After we had paid deposits and three months advance rental on our two new flats, and paid for the furniture we'd bought from La Samaritaine, we had a total of $46,000 left from the $100,000 that the Colonel (via Vernon) had given us as cash. At that time, in 1978, a dollar was worth about four and a half French francs and so we had just over 200,000 in French francs available in cash. We were committed to pay around 3,000 francs a month each in rent and our living costs were probably the same again. It didn't take me long with a calculator to work out that in a year and a half we would run out of money. We would be broke. We would have fairly substantial commitments but we would have zero income. And, as Charles Dickens' Mr Micawber was so fond of pointing out, a man whose expenditure exceeds his income is heading straight for financial disaster.

'We have two choices,' I told Elvis. 'We can try to find jobs so that we can make the remaining cash last longer or we can take a risk and invest some of the money we have in a business.' We were sitting in Elvis's new flat. It looked very elegant. The woman in the green dress, whose name turned out to be Fabrianne, had just left. Elvis had to zip her into the dress. There had been several cuddles, many kisses and a promise to meet again that evening.

'She seems like a nice lady.'

'She is. She likes Englishmen.'

'Good. She believes you're English.'

'Oh yes.'

I wasn't surprised. Elvis had done well at picking up English slang, English idioms and English words that were alternative to American words. He often called me 'dear old thing', referred to trousers as trousers rather than as 'pants' and never referred to toilettes as 'rest rooms'. He even spoke with a half way decent English accent. He had lost the famous Mississippi drawl.

'She seems to speak good English.'

'She's French but she's married to an American. I don't know what he does but he apparently spends a lot of time doing it. She's very lonely. She's promised to help me with my French.'

I nodded. Elvis's French was improving rapidly though his vocabulary was stronger in the area of romance than in dealing with blocked drains, plumbers and such things. He could flirt and flatter as well as any Frenchman but I still had to sort out the dull stuff. I didn't mind.

'She has a friend who's divorced,' said Elvis. 'We could fix up an evening together. The four of us.'

'Are you trying to set me up with a blind date?'

'Do you good. You might like her. Fabrianne says she's good looking and runs a bakery. She's quite rich.'

'Maybe,' I agreed with less reluctance than I had expected to hear myself offer.

'Plenty of dough,' said Elvis.

I looked at him.

He apologised. '

'We need to decide what we're going to do.'

'What sort of jobs can we get?'

'Nothing very grand. We don't have any qualifications and we still have the problem that neither of us has experience we can talk about.'

'So, what do you think?'

'We'd be lucky to get jobs as labourers. We almost certainly wouldn't get jobs as waiters.'

Hildy the cat jumped onto Elvis's lap. We had decided that she could spend half her life living in my apartment and half living in Elvis's. It would give her a bit of variety.

'I can earn some money busking,' said Elvis.

I shook my head. 'It's too risky,' I pointed out. 'And if the police pick you up and finger-print you then we're finished.'

'I could try to get a job as a session musician, backing vocals, playing guitar.'

'That would be asking for trouble. You'd be working with professional musicians. How long do you think you would last before someone spotted you?'

Glumly, Elvis agreed with me.

'That leaves us with the second alternative.'

'Run a business.'

'Exactly.'

'It's the only real option isn't it?'

'I think so.'

'So, what sort of business can we run?'

'We could start a newspaper or magazine.'

'I like that. We were doing OK until Hildy died.' Elvis's face lit up. 'You can write the words and I can take the pictures.'

'A little magazine for expats might work. But we'd have to make it monthly. Weekly is too much.'

'Agreed.'

'Or we could open a pub or café for Brits. Ye Olde English Tea Shoppe. When the English have been away from home for an hour or two they become maudlin and painfully patriotic; they crave cups of tea, plates of fish and chips and pints of warm beer; they desperately need Cooper's marmalade, Marmite and baked beans on toast. At home they probably avoid these iconic English staples; preferring pasta, curry and hot dogs. But abroad they cannot manage without them. Spanish holiday resorts which are popular with British holidaymakers are awash with English Pubs, fish and chip shops and cafés selling tea and crumpets served on gingham clothed tables by waitresses in frilly edged pinafores.

Elvis screwed up his nose. 'Do you know anything about running a café?'

'No. But I've been in loads of them. How hard can it be? Make tea, put it in cups and sell it for 200 times as much as you paid for it.'

'What about a club?' asked Elvis, who was clearly not excited by the prospect of spending the next few years serving seed cake and cucumber sandwiches. 'There's too much competition in the café business. We could open a club in St Germain. Down by the river somewhere. There are loads of students looking for somewhere to go in the evenings. Some of the girls are very pretty when they've had a good wash.'

'Students don't have much money and for a club we need too many staff. We would need licences and performers and we'd have to work 18 hours a day.'

'Perhaps not a club then,' said Elvis quickly. I knew that he would not be keen on a job which would take up too much time. It would cut into his all-important love life.

We both thought for a while. Hildy stood up, turned round three times, licked his or her bottom, scratched an ear and then lay down again. He or she had settled in very well.

'What about a record shop?' asked Elvis. 'Just selling British and American artists.'

'That might work,' I agreed. I thought about it. 'I like that idea very much.'

'We could have a second hand section where we sold stuff that was difficult to find.'

'I do like that idea,' I told him. 'There are plenty of small shops available to rent. We need to be in St Germain – where the musicians and students congregate.'

'What shall we call it?' asked Elvis.

'Vinyl and Tape?'

'I like that.'

'Or we could just call it 'The Music Shop'.'

'In English?'

'Yes. The French like British and American music. They'd know what it meant.'

'But they might think we were selling sheet music and instruments. Do we want to sell sheet music and instruments?'

'No, I don't think so. We'd need a massive shop to display violins and tubas, let alone pianos and drum kits. Let's specialise in selling records.'

'On vinyl and tape.'

'Exactly. Vinyl and Tape.' I looked at him. 'Lots of girls buy records,' I said.

'I know,' he grinned.

'We could go over to London and pick up records there. There are tons of stalls selling records around London. Petticoat Lane. Portobello Road.'

'We'd need a van.'

'I wonder what happened to Hildy's old van?'

'I'm not driving to London in that!'

'I bet it's still where it was. Parked in the courtyard. She didn't know Hildy had a van. The notaire didn't know.'

'We don't have the keys.'

'We do,' I told him. 'I gave the flat keys to Hildy's sister but I forgot to give her the van keys. I've got them in a drawer somewhere.'

Fifty five minutes later we were driving Hildy's old Citroen up the Rue de Bellchasse. We parked it with two wheels on the road and two on the pavement. What did we care if a French meter maid slapped a ticket underneath the windscreen wiper? Until we reregistered the van it was still in Hildy's name. And Hildy wasn't going to worry about a few parking tickets.

Chapter Forty Three

Two weeks later we walked away from an estate agent's office with the keys for our new shop in my pocket. We'd found premises in St Germain and we'd paid the rent for the first six months tenancy. The place was perfect; small enough to be beguiling but larger than it looked at first. There were two first floor rooms we could use as offices and storage and a cellar we could use if we needed to expand at some time in the future. (Elvis suggested that we call this part of the shop The Cavern, after the cellar club in Liverpool where the Beatles had so famously performed.) The place was filthy and we needed to find and fit shelving and racks for the display of the records and tapes we were hoping to sell but the position was as good as we could possibly get. We were in Rue Danton, a popularly used street near to the Sorbonne and we could expect to attract quite a bit of passing tourist traffic, in addition to the students who we hoped would be our main customer base.

We wandered into a large and enormously popular café on the Boulevard Saint Michel to celebrate the beginning of new venture. Elvis ordered a cappuccino and I ordered a peppermint tea. It was a gloriously warm day, too hot for vin chaud.

At a nearby table a group of students had pulled together half a dozen tables. They were sitting quietly, occasionally chatting to one another but mainly staring at a single white candle in a simple candlestick in front of them. It looked like a wake.

'Has a student died?' I asked our waiter when he brought our drinks.

'Non, non,' said the waiter, shaking his head. 'Il est aujourd'hui un an depuis la mort du roi.' It is a year today since the king died.

'Le roi?' I said, puzzled.

'Elvis,' said the waiter. 'Elvis Presley est mort il ya un an aujourd'hui.' Elvis died a year ago today.

I looked again at the table with the candle and this time I saw a picture of Elvis standing next to the candle. I then looked at the calendar clock behind the bar. It was, indeed, the 16th August. It was scarcely believable that our Great Adventure had begun just twelve months earlier. So much had happened. We had been in Paris for no more than nine months. Altogether, it had been by far the most dramatic year of my life.

I looked across at Elvis. He was sipping his coffee and watching the students.

'It must feel strange,' I said.

'Not really.' Elvis took another sip at the coffee. 'If Elvis hadn't died then his image would have been destroyed completely. He should have gone ten years earlier.' It did not escape me that it was the first time I had ever heard him refer to 'Elvis' in the third person. It wasn't an affectation, in the way that Jerry Lee Lewis referred to himself in the third person, it was a recognition that Elvis was another person, someone who had lived in another country, in another time.

'Ten years?'

'Maybe five,' laughed Elvis. He finished his coffee.

One of the students had a guitar. He started singing 'Love Me Tender'. He didn't have a bad voice. Several of the girls and one of the boys were crying.

'Shall we go?' asked Elvis. He stood up and tucked a twenty franc note under his cup to pay for our drinks. It was far too much but although he was doing well with the language Elvis still hadn't sorted out the currency.

'Where to?' I asked him.

'We need to buy some brooms and start clearing out our new shop,' he said. 'It's filthy dirty and it's not going to clean itself.'

And so that was what we did. Our second year in Paris, and the second year of the Great Adventure, was about to commence.

Printed in Great Britain
by Amazon